"Welcome to the first dictionary ____ finish. *The Da Vinci Code Break____* readable—overview of the names, facts, dates, and everything else you need to know about *The Da Vinci Code*."

—Ted Haggard, Senior Pastor, New Life Church
President, National Association of Evangelicals

"
"

"*The Da Vinci Code* reminds us once again how much interest people have in the story of Jesus. Curiosity about who he was and what he did never seems to come to an end. In a work like *The Da Vinci Code*, fiction can be easily confused as an accurate portrayal of history. In this case, the facts about Jesus are far more amazing than anything we could make up or imagine. Jim Garlow provides for us a great glossary to help us unwrap the amazing mystery that goes far beyond *The Da Vinci Code*."

—Erwin Raphael McManus, Lead Pastor, Mosaic

"
"

"Jim Garlow's previously coauthored book on *The Da Vinci Code* "led the pack" both in timing and sales as well as in content. Now comes a badly needed tool, a dictionary that helps every *Da Vinci Code* reader understand the real meaning of terms that Dan Brown used, plus provides so many words or concepts that should have been in *The Da Vinci Code*, but were omitted. *The Da Vinci Code Breaker* is a badly needed historical corrective to *The Da Vinci Code* errors."

—Jack Hayford, Founding Pastor, The Church on the Way
Founder and Chancellor, King's College and Seminary

"
"

"Satan always aims his big guns at the doctrine of the Trinity. If Jesus is not divine, then he could not have paid for our sins and our faith is in vain. Jim Garlow (along with Peter Jones) has provided such an excellent rebuttal in *Cracking Da Vinci's Code*. Now [Garlow] has provided another helpful book, *The Da Vinci Code Breaker*, to help counter the lies propagated by this blockbuster book and movie."

—D. James Kennedy, Ph.D., Senior Minister, Coral Ridge Presbyterian Church

AN **EASY-TO-USE** FACT CHECKER

THE
DAVINCI
CODEBREAKER

JAMES L. GARLOW

WITH TIMOTHY PAUL JONES AND APRIL WILLIAMS

BETHANYHOUSE
MINNEAPOLIS, MINNESOTA

Published by Bethany House Publishers
11400 Hampshire Avenue South
Bloomington, Minnesota 55438

Bethany House Publishers is a division of
Baker Publishing Group, Grand Rapids, Michigan.

Printed in the United States of America

ISBN-13: 978-0-7642-0185-1
ISBN-10: 0-7642-0185-9

Library of Congress Cataloging-in-Publication Data

Garlow, James L.
      The Da Vinci codebreaker : an easy-to-use fact checker for truth seekers / James L.
Garlow.
            p.   cm.
      Summary: "An exposé of the bestselling novel. Readers questioning The Da Vinci Code
can 'fact check' with this book of terms, events, people and places"—Provided by publisher.
      ISBN 0-7642-0185-9 (pbk.)
      1. Brown, Dan, 1964- Da Vinci code—Dictionaries.   2. Mary Magdalene, Saint—In
literature—Dictionaries.   3. Jesus Christ—In literature—Dictionaries.   4. Christianity in
literature—Dictionaries.   I. Title.
      PS3552.R685434D33385   2006
      813'.54—dc22

                                                                          2005032604

Dedicated by Jim, Timothy, and April
to a Band of Brothers . . . and Sisters too

Jim . . .
Janie Garlow
Judy Garlow Wade
Bob Garlow
Bill Garlow

Timothy . . .
Debra Jones Eden
Pamela Jones Kirk
Shyre Jones McCune
Kevin Jones
James Jones

April . . .
Shannon Boyd

ACKNOWLEDGMENTS

I am deeply indebted to my two wonderful coauthors:

• Timothy Paul Jones
• April Williams.

They did such outstanding and voluminous work that they morphed from research assistants to coauthors. Timothy and April were steady "we-can-do-this-so-let's-stay-at-it" people. They were the exact type of colleague needed for such a project.

This is only one of many of Timothy's writings. The caliber and quality of his contribution is demonstrated by his exceptional chart included in the "New Testament canon" entry.

This is April's first book, and far from her last.

I could not have done this without them.

To both of you, I say an enormous heartfelt "thank you."

Others assisted at various stages in varying ways:

• Dr. Gerard Reed, author and professor at Point Loma Nazarene University, has worked with me before on book projects. He keeps a cool head under the greatest time constraints.
• Dr. Peter Jones, international lecturer, author, and professor at Westminster Theological Seminary, was my coauthor on *Cracking Da Vinci's Code*. Even after working and traveling together, we managed to remain the best of friends. And when together, we laugh very hard.
• Dr. Michael Christenson, author and professor at Drew University, is a long-term friend with whom I love to argue. Holding several different opinions has somehow caused us to enjoy our brief times together even more. I know I could turn to him for help anytime—and I did!
• Dr. Franco Morando, associate professor of Italian studies and chair, Department of Romance Languages & Literatures, Boston College, responded with only a moment's notice, and gracefully jumped in to help me. His expertise is known far and wide.

- Fr. John C. Vargas, Roman Catholic priest of the Redemptorists Order (The Congregation of the Most Holy Redeemer) of the Alphonsian Academy of Moral Theology, Rome, Italy, graciously examined the manuscript with superbly helpful suggestions and encouragement. He gave me a distinct perspective that my Protestant background would not have afforded.
- Professor Richard Howard, whose brilliance is evidenced by his doctoral studies at Harvard, kindly assisted. He was willing to look at the manuscript and once again become "Prof," as he was decades before when I was his college student. At eighty-six his body is confined behind his walker in the retirement home, but his mind is keen as ever. Thank you, "Prof," once more.

I am so grateful for Kyle Duncan of Bethany House, who has encouraged, cheered, and advised me about several writing projects with the grace and dignity of a true Christian gentleman. He is both a friend in "book-writing" and a confidant in "life-living."

When an author acknowledges his or her spouse and children, he or she does not do so out of a sense of duty. It is done because families pay a price when a book is written. Words cannot express the support I have from my wife, my four children, my son in-law, my daughter-in-law, my grandchildren, and my extended family. To Carol, Janie and Jeremy, Josh and Lacy, Jacob, Josie, Riley, Aidan, Lukas, Jackson, Winifred, Keat and Judy, Bill and Laurie, I say a heartfelt "thank you."

To Shadow, the family dog, I say "stop barking." I will now spend more time with you.

Jim Garlow
San Diego, March 2006

QUOTES ABOUT
DAN BROWN'S
THE DA VINCI CODE

"I found The Da Vinci Code *much more offensive as a scholar than as a believer."*
  —Gary A. Byers, Executive Director of the Associates for Biblical Research and Administrative Director of the Ai Expedition at Khirbet el-Maqatir in Israel ("The Historical Basis of Dan Brown's *The Da Vinci Code*" at *http://aftrain.com/arc/2004/davinci.htm.*)

"
"

"The writer gives the impression that he's also a historian—which he is not. I don't think he's so much interested in the truth as in drama and mystery."
  —Jack Wasserman, retired professor of art history, expert on Leonardo da Vinci, Temple University, Philadelphia (Patrick T. Reardon, *"'The Da Vinci Code'... Unscrambled."* 2/5/04: *Chicago Tribune,* A1.)

"
"

"For storytelling I give it an A, [for] knowledge of the history of theology and history of the church, C-minus, [for] systematic theology ... an F."
  —James Halstead, Chairman of the Religious Studies Department at DePaul University (Patrick T. Reardon, *"'The Da Vinci Code'... Unscrambled."* 2/5/04: *Chicago Tribune,* A1.)

"
"

"Just about everything [Dan Brown] says about Leonardo da Vinci is wrong."
  —Jack Wasserman, retired professor of art history, expert on Leonardo da Vinci, Temple University, Philadelphia (Patrick T. Reardon, *"'The Da Vinci Code'... Unscrambled."* 2/5/04: *Chicago Tribune,* A1.)

HOW
THE DA VINCI CODE BREAKER
CAME TO BE

This is not a foreword because in my opinion people (at least some) do not read forewords. Treat this section as chapter 1. It's critical that you see how and why this book came to be.

Every book has a story, and this one is no exception; a book tends to be more valuable if its readers know that story. In order to tell the story of *this* book, I must tell you the story of one that came before it.

I knew something was wrong when Priscilla greeted me that morning with urgency. "My brother-in-law has just read a book attacking the Bible and Jesus, and he believes the book."

"What book?" I asked.

"*The Da Vinci Code!*" she exclaimed. "Furthermore, it claims that Jesus was married to Mary Magdalene and that they had a child."

I'd never heard of *The Da Vinci Code,* which was just starting to be noted by the reading public. "If it's a novel, don't worry about it. No one will ever believe it!"

I was wrong.

The Da Vinci Code exploded around the world, selling well over 40 million copies in forty-three languages and resulting in a major motion picture. More than merely *a* bestseller, it became *the* bestselling adult novel of all time.

In the weeks that followed, I encountered more people with friends and family who believed the historical and theological concepts in Dan Brown's book. These people were said to be willing to abandon their Christian faith in favor of the core themes of a *novel.*

Then came Jeff's call. Jeff had been the editor of a book I'd written on the Muslim faith, *A Christian's Response to Islam* (Cook, 2002), and now he too had urgency in his voice: "Jim, you have to write a book responding to *The Da Vinci Code!*" I informed him that while honored to be asked, I was not the right guy. But two more calls followed within twenty-four hours, both with the same intensity: "You must write a response."

It was the third call that caused me to hesitantly consider. When I explained that I would need a research assistant, a quick call to my friend Peter Jones revealed that he too had been approached to write on the topic. "Let's coauthor a book," he suggested. I was overjoyed to work with him.

Within a couple of weeks, Peter, Jeff, and I met in a hotel room for two days, outlining key issues to be addressed. A few weeks later *Cracking Da Vinci's Code* (Cook, 2004) was on the shelves, and we were off to New York City for interviews at CNN and Fox. A front page *New York Times* article (4/27/04) would open doors to every major national news outlet—we ended up with more than a dozen national TV appearances, countless radio interviews, and dialogues with national magazines and foreign newspapers. Meanwhile, *Cracking Da Vinci's Code* hit #17 on the *New York Times* Bestseller List (Paperback—Nonfiction), #96 on the *USA TODAY* Top 150 Bestseller List, and #4 among inspirational books in Wal-Mart stores.

While this response indicated widespread desire to know more about Dan Brown's *Da Vinci Code* claims, our book signings were even more revealing. The recipient would lean over and say, "I'm getting this book for my . . ." (son or daughter, father or mother, nephew or niece, or *someone*). The next phrase was one I heard hundreds of times: "He (or she) believes *The Da Vinci Code*." This only confirmed what had compelled us to write in the first place.

Radio interviews confirmed the same—when hosts opened the lines for questions, callers repeatedly referred to those who believed Dan Brown's book. One host began chiding me, "Why on earth did you write a book against a *novel*?" When he prodded a third time, almost mockingly, I asked him if he'd read it. Hesitantly, he admitted he hadn't.

Brown's writing style mixes fact (very little) with fiction (very much) in such a way that the uninitiated cannot distinguish between them; I call this style "fact-ion." When I was interviewed by Linda Vester on Fox's *DaySide* show, a guest with an opposing view scoffed at the notion of people failing to sort out fact from fiction. Vester turned to her studio audience and asked,

"How many of you have read *The Da Vinci Code*?"

Many hands went up. She looked at a woman near her and asked, "Could you tell the difference between fact and fiction when you read it?"

"Absolutely not," the woman forcefully responded.

My point exactly.

To help people sort fact from fiction, accurate definitions were needed for the terms used in (and related to) *The Da Vinci Code*. I originally wanted to include a glossary in the back of *Cracking Da Vinci's Code*, but as every author knows, time (deadlines) and space (allotted pages) are often enemies of the writer who has more to say. With the passage of time, hundreds of conversations, radio interviews, and media buzz persuaded me that a glossary was still badly needed. Thus *The Da Vinci Code Breaker* was born.

Allow me to make a disclaimer: This book is not about bashing Dan Brown. Frankly, I think his novelist's skills are strong, and I found his writing to be a true page-turner—I read straight through, finishing at five in the morning.

Furthermore, as a courtesy, we tried to contact him before we wrote *Cracking Da Vinci's Code*. His publicist would not allow any contact.

Dan Brown could have spared himself the critical barrage from historians, theologians, and art experts of all persuasions. He invited ridicule when his opening page began with the word *FACT* and then proceeded to expound fiction. Even more ludicrous is his claim that "all descriptions of artwork, architecture, documents, and secret rituals in this novel are accurate." If he would have said that "all descriptions of artwork, architecture, documents, and secret rituals in this novel are fictional," almost no one would have taken issue with him.

If Brown had simply come forward and stated that his book is a novel and that as fiction it should not be taken seriously with regard to history, theology, and art, he would not have created the (admittedly lucrative) consequent firestorm. Or if he had come forward in a timely manner and acknowledged that it contains a myriad of significant errors, serious thinkers would have been very forgiving. Book errors are common—I've found post-publication errors in every book I've written, even though editors and proofreaders have gone to great lengths to locate and correct errors before the first printing. I suspect that we'll have to make corrections in later editions of this book as well.

But rather than admitting that his book is fiction or contains many errors, Brown defended it as being accurate, triggering an avalanche of merited anti-*Da Vinci Code* media—articles, books, DVDs, even television shows.

Foolishly, when provided opportunities to speak, Brown dug himself yet deeper. On *Today* with Matt Lauer, when asked if the novel was based on "things that actually occurred," Brown responded, "Absolutely all of it. Obviously . . . Robert Langdon is fictional, but all of the art, architecture, secret rituals, secret societies, all of that is historical fact."

What is one to conclude?

- Is Brown so unskilled as to do such shoddy historical work and not realize it? Unlikely. He seems extremely bright.
- Is it possible that Brown uses the status of his work as fiction so that he can regard historical accuracy as unimportant? No—he has firmly defended it as "historical fact."

What possibilities remain? There are two, both with the same inflection:

- That he intentionally misled by mishandling data. If so, why? The only probable answer would be that Brown wrote *The Da Vinci Code* with an agenda: to convince his reader of something, whether or not it's true.
- That he truly believes what he wrote and that he also has the aforementioned agenda.

If Brown has an agenda, what is it? *To destroy, as best he can, the credibility of orthodox Christianity by refuting two themes: the authenticity and reliability of the New Testament and the full divinity of Jesus.* Overarching both is the redefinition of God; this was first pointed out to me by Peter Jones. God, to Dan Brown, is not the transcendent, above-and-beyond God portrayed in the Bible. God is creation itself—something within me. It (god) is, in fact, me. I don't look to the Bible for truth. I simply look within.

In one sense, *The Da Vinci Code* has done Christianity and the Bible a great favor, sparking questions believers should have been asking and answering long before reading about "the code." If people will seriously examine the historical data, they will know what they believe and why they believe it. For example, they will discover the monumental evidence for the reliability and authenticity of the Old and New Testaments, along with the historical verifiability for the resurrection of Jesus. Dan Brown is not to be feared but cheered. When people are truly open to honest exploration, orthodox Christianity fares well.

Does Brown succeed in making his case through *The Da Vinci Code*? If he does, his facts, sources, and terms must be accurate. To determine this, turn the page and read the following glossary of terms, concepts, and persons that either are included in *The Da Vinci Code* or should have been included.

"
    "

Author's note: All citations from *The Da Vinci Code* (*DVC*) refer to page numbers in the originally published hardcover edition (Doubleday, 2003).

Abanes, Richard Author of *The Truth Behind the Da Vinci Code*.

Acts of Andrew, The Late-second- or early-third-century Christian document; supposed account of the apostle Andrew's missionary journeys and martyrdom (in Achaia [southern Greece] and Scythia [Ukraine, southern Russia]). *Acts of Andrew* seems to have utilized *Acts of John* and *Acts of Peter* as sources; it may have come from the same author, who was certainly not an eyewitness of first-century events. Although popular among some ancient and medieval Christians, no early Christian writer considered this document to have any authority for believers or any place among the canonical Scriptures. See also apocrypha; canon.

Acts of John, The Mid-second-century docetic writing; supposed account of two journeys by the apostle John to Ephesus; includes an ancient tradition, also preserved in Tertullian's third-century writings, that Roman Emperor Domitian (r. 81–96) had John thrown in a vat of boiling oil, which the apostle survived. *The Acts of John* never claims to have been written by an apostle, and it includes several docetic comments, that is, remarks seeming to deny Christ's full humanity: "Sometimes when I touched Jesus," John allegedly claims at one point, "his substance was immaterial . . . as if it did not exist at all." The docetic statements appear in the Greek manuscripts of *The Acts of John* but not in any Latin texts. Although the Latin manuscripts were copied later, it is possible that they reflect an earlier manuscript tradition in which docetic elements were absent. No early Christian writer considered *The Acts of John* to have any authority for believers or any place among the canonical Scriptures. See also canon; Docetism; Gnosticism.

Acts of Paul, The Mid-second-century Christian writing; supposed account of the apostle Paul's missionary travels. Only two-thirds of this document survive, primarily in three other texts: *Corinthians, Third, The Acts of Paul and Thecla,* and *The Martyrdom of Paul.* According to Tertullian (*De Baptismo* 17:5), a church leader in Asia Minor admitted around AD 160 that he had authored *Acts of Paul;* he said that the writing was primarily fictional but that he did it "out of respect for Paul." The book was never considered for inclusion in the New Testament canon, but Thecla's martyrdom may have actually occurred; several Christian writers, including Eusebius ("father of church history") and Augustine (most influential early Christian leader), refer to it. See also *Corinthians, Third; Acts of Paul and Thecla;* Augustine of Hippo; canon; Eusebius of Caesarea; Tertullian of Carthage.

Acts of Paul and Thecla, The Mid-second-century Christian writing; supposed account of the apostle Paul's preaching and the martyrdom of a virgin named Thecla; Paul is depicted throughout as proclaiming a negative view of marriage and sexual pleasure. Most remarkable for containing the earliest known description of Paul's physical characteristics: "A man small in size, baldheaded, bowlegged, of noble appearance, with eyebrows meeting, and a rather hooked nose. Yet he was full of grace; sometimes he seemed like a man, and sometimes he had the face of an angel." *The Acts of Paul and Thecla* was part of the larger *Acts of Paul.* See *Acts of Paul.*

Acts of Peter, The Late-second-century Christian writing; based on the earlier *Acts of John;* narrates a fictionalized "miracle contest" between Simon Peter and the magician Simon Magus (contrast with Acts 8). The concluding chapters, which seem at some point to have circulated separately from the rest of the document, describe Peter's death by upside-down crucifixion; these chapters may represent an authentic tradition as to his execution. Nevertheless, no early Christian writer considered *Acts of Peter* to have any place among the canonical Scriptures, possibly because it could not be clearly connected to an eyewitness. See also canon.

Acts of Pilate, The Early-fourth-century forgeries of a supposed report by Pontius Pilate to Emperor Tiberius. There are actually two *Acts of Pilate*—one by Emperor Maximian (r. 285–310) to discredit Christianity, another by an anonymous Christian to discredit Pontius Pilate. Both works are clearly false. No early Christian writer considered either of these documents to have any authority for believers or any place among the canonical Scriptures. See canon.

Acts of Thomas, The Late-second- or early-third-century Gnostic writing; supposed account of the apostle Thomas's missionary journey and martyrdom in India; claims to have been written by Thomas, yet its grammatical style and known history reveal an origin at least a century after the apostles' deaths. The theology is clearly Gnostic—i.e., one's salvation comes by attaining certain "higher knowledge" and rejecting the material (tangible) in favor of the metaphysical (intangible); this is especially evident in its negative view of marriage and sexuality. Sexual pleasure, even in the context of a loving marriage, is described as "lasciviousness and bitterness of soul." Thomas's martyrdom may have an authentic historical tradition, but no early Christian writer considered *Acts of Thomas* to have any authority for believers or any place among the canonical Scriptures. See also canon; Gnosticism.

AD Abbreviation for the Latin *Anno Domini,* "The Lord's Year" or "The Year of Our Lord"; a calendar designation intended to represent the number of years since the birth of Jesus. When calculating the date for Easter in 525, Dionysius Exiguus, a monastic scholar, established that year as the five hundred and twenty-fifth since Christ's birth. Unfortunately, his calculations were a bit imprecise—as it happens, he was off by approximately four years. Thus, Jesus was probably born in 4 BC—four years before the year Exiguus designated as AD 1. See also BC; BCE; CE.

Adonai Hebrew title for *Supreme Lord,* designated by the letters *YHWH,* or, popularly, *Yahweh* (*YHWH* is also known as the *Tetragrammaton*). The Jews used *Adonai* as a substitute for God's name, which they fervently believed should be reverenced by not being spoken aloud. That *Adonai* is technically the plural form of *Adoni* does not imply that there is more than one God; its usage may be what is termed "plural of majesty," similar to a person of earthly royalty referring to himself with the plural *we* instead of singular *I.* See also *Jehovah; YHWH.*

Adoptionism The belief that Jesus was an ordinary human who became the

Son of God at his baptism. Early Christians rejected Adoptionism because it contradicts New Testament teaching; according to John 1:1, Jesus ("the Word") was divine from "the beginning." John the Baptist (a cousin of Jesus who announced the Messiah's coming) and Jesus himself testified that he existed before his earthly birth. (cf. John 1:15; 8:58). See also Christology.

Adoration of the Magi Although Leonardo da Vinci never finished this 1481–82 painting (his services were wanted by the Duke of Milan), it is considered one of his more important early works. *Adoration* is especially intriguing because it has an earlier drawing under the visible artwork; to Dan Brown, this evidences a conspiracy to hide the "original" drawing, which he believes might contain clues to information that would damage the church. In reality, leaving the visible painting was not done "to subvert Da Vinci's true intention" (*DVC,* 169). Resistance to restoring *Adoration* to its "hidden" under-drawing was about leaving it in its rightful state—as Leonardo left it.

Aeon Greek word that means "ever-existing," referring to an age (or ages) wherein the material world proceeded or evolved by "emanations." A favorite second-century Gnostic term; to Valentinus, for example, the *Aeon* emanated from a divine substance coeternal with God. In refutation, Irenaeus said, "They maintain . . . that in the invisible and ineffable heights above there exists a certain perfect, pre-existent Aeon . . . invisible and incomprehensible" (*Against Heresies,* I.1.316). Gnostics constructed a convoluted cosmic scheme wherein a variety of deities played a role in creating the material world, thus effectively denying that God personally created the heavens and the earth. See Gnosticism; Valentinus.

Age of Aquarius, The Aquarius, meaning "water-bearer," is one of the twelve signs of the zodiac; *The Da Vinci Code* describes the Age of Aquarius as the coming era in which the Roman Catholic Church foresees a shift in human attitude and behavior to reflect the sign (*DVC,* 268). Qualities of the zodiacal Aquarius include self-reliance, free thinking, and a peaceful mindset. Some believe the Age of Aquarius began at the dawn of the Third Millennium (i.e., 2000); however, according to calculations from a variety of contemporary astrologers, this age will begin in the twenty-seventh century, or at least six hundred years from now. See also Age of Pisces; astrology; zodiac.

Age of Pisces, The Greek, *fish;* since from ancient times the fish has been used as a Christian symbol, some see the arrival of the Aquarian Age as signaling the passing of Christianity. *The Da Vinci Code* describes the current Piscean Age as one of passivity—accordingly, Dan Brown says, people have been easily controlled by the Roman Catholic Church for the past two thousand years (*DVC,* 267). See also Age of Aquarius; astrology; zodiac.

Albigensian Crusade, The The Cathari were a religious sect in a region known as Languedoc, in present-day southern France. The term *Albigensian* arose from the crusaders' assumption that the Cathari were concentrated in the village of Albi (ancient Albiga). Pope Innocent III declared the Crusade (roughly 1208–1229) allegedly to eradicate the Cathar heresy. See also Cathari.

alchemy An unsystematic mixture of scientific and unscientific research and methods, including chemistry, physics, and medicine alongside astrology, spiritualism, and mysticism; a precursor to later scientific disciplines (a protoscience). Originating in the ancient East and Near East, alchemy (*DVC,* 45) later found fertile ground in the West and was taken seriously in Europe up to the Enlightenment. In the East, alchemy has been intertwined with Taoism; in the West, alchemy heavily influenced the beginning and development of Rosicrucianism and has impacted both Kabbalism and cryptography.

Some Western alchemists were pseudo-practitioners whose main designs were to create magic potions and turn common elements into gold and silver; others were sincere learners who sought to understand difficult subjects through investigation and exploration. See also astrology; cryptography; Kabbalah; modernity; postmodernity; Rosicrucians.

Alexander VI, Pope (r. 1492–1503) The memorably decadent Rodrigo Borgia (given name) was a financial supporter of Leonardo da Vinci. Perhaps the most corrupt of the Renaissance popes, Alexander VI became a cardinal at age twenty-nine and lived a notoriously licentious life, siring six or more illegitimate children (including Caesar Borgia, brutal commander of the papal army). Some believe he became pope by bribing the electors; as a pope who lived luxuriously, he also spent vast sums on building projects in Rome. See also Renaissance.

Alexander the Great Macedonian ruler; d. 323 BC; also known as Alexander III and Alexander of Macedon. King of Macedon, a state comprising portions of present-day Greece, and conqueror of much of the ancient world; at the time of his death, around the young age of thirty-two, Alexander's kingdom stretched from Greece to India. The son of King Philip II, Alexander received his education from Aristotle, who convinced him that Greek culture represented the absolute epitome of progress; Alexander subsequently spread Greek culture throughout the lands he subdued. See also Hellenism; Hellenization.

allegory Though many Christian exegetes (e.g., Ambrose and Augustine) have employed allegorical methods to plumb the Bible's spiritual depths, Dan Brown views allegory as a variety of "imagining that it's so makes it so," a make-your-own-reality approach. This parallels the biblical approach of Rudolph Bultmann, an influential German scholar who endeavored to "demythologize" Scripture and make it palatable to moderns. Thus, allegedly, the Resurrection never happened, but Christ's disciples were so thrilled with his influence that they spoke and wrote as if it were factually true.

Brown suggests that believing the illusion "helps millions of people cope and be better people" (*DVC*, 342). Summing up Christian beliefs, Robert Langdon leads Sophie Neveu to conclude: "It appears that their reality is false."

Alpha Galates French nationalist organization; name means "First Gauls"; established in 1942 by Pierre Plantard, who later made false claims about his ties to royalty and also falsified documents to appear that the Priory of Sion was a centuries-old secret organization. See Plantard, Pierre.

Amon Egyptian god; also spelled *Amun* and *Amen*. According to *The Da Vinci Code*, the name of Leonardo's *Mona Lisa* is an anagram of *Amon* and *L'isa*—Egyptian deities that allegedly represented male and female fertility. Building on this thesis, Dan Brown claims that Leonardo intended the person portrayed in the painting to be androgynous (with both male and female characteristics), and that this depiction represents Leonardo's own sexuality.

This approach is riddled with errors. First, *L'isa* is not an alternate spelling of the goddess name *Isis* (as Brown says; *DVC,* 120). Second, Amon was god of the air, not of fertility, and Amon's consort was Mut, not Isis. (The consort of Isis was Osiris.) Third, the painting known in the English-speaking world as *Mona Lisa* was never known as such in its native country or its current country of residence; to this day it's referred to as *La Gioconda* in Italy and as *La Joconde* in France. See also Isis; Leonardo da Vinci; L'isa; *Mona Lisa.*

anagram A word or phrase created by transposing the letters of another word or phrase, such as occurs when the characters of *O, Draconian devil!* are rearranged to become *Leonardo da Vinci!* or when the letters of *Baigent*—last name of an author of *Holy Blood, Holy Grail*—are rearranged to spell *Teabing,* surname of a key *Da Vinci Code* figure (*DVC,* 98).

ankh A cross with a ring at the top stake (shorter end); term comes from the Egyptian hieroglyphic for *life.* Some suggest that Christians later borrowed this imagery to associate Christ's cross with new birth or new life; the ankh is more generally associated with Wiccan worship. The cross's lower portion is associated with masculinity, while the upper portion, or circle, is associated with femininity.

Aphrodite See Venus/Aphrodite.

Apocalypse of Paul, The Late-fourth-century Christian writing; also known as *The Vision of Paul;* a reworking of *Apocalypse of Peter* that claimed to have been unearthed in Cilicia of Tarsus, the apostle Paul's hometown. The ancient church historian Sozomen (d. c. 447) investigated this claim and found evidence that the document had originated during the reign of Emperor Theodosius I (r. 378–395); Paul clearly didn't write it. One variant copy, known as *The Apocalypse of the Virgin,* replaces Paul with Mary, mother of Jesus. No early Christian writer considered either work to have any authority for believers or any place among the New Testament Scriptures. (*The Apocalypse of Paul* is frequently confused with *The Coptic Apocalypse of Paul.*) See also apostle; canon; *Coptic Apocalypse of Paul.*

Apocalypse of Peter, The Second-century Christian document; also known as *The Revelation to Peter.* Cited as Scripture by Clement of Alexandria and in the Muratorian Fragment, but although nothing in it contradicts the canonical New Testament, it was ultimately excluded for two reasons: (1) It was written around 135, so Simon Peter (who died c. 66) didn't write it, and New Testament documents had to be connected to an apostolic eyewitness. (2) It sometimes circulated with a docetic writing known as the *Gospel of Peter* (*Apocalypse of Peter* is frequently confused with *The Coptic Apocalypse of Peter,* a Gnostic text found at Nag Hammadi). See also apostle; canon; Clement of Alexandria; *Coptic Apocalypse of Paul; Coptic Apocalypse of Peter;* Docetism; Gnosticism; *Gospel of Peter;* Muratorian Fragment; Nag Hammadi.

apocalyptic From Greek *apokalypsis,* meaning "revelation" or "unveiling"; a class of literature popular in the centuries-long era following the sixth-century-BC Jewish exile to Babylon. Examples include the biblical books of Daniel and Revelation and such non-biblical books as *The Apocalypse of Paul, The Apocalypse of Peter,* and *Shepherd of Hermas.* Apocalyptic literature typically includes (1) the revealing of a mystery beyond normal human knowledge; (2) a dream or vision; (3) angelic beings; (4) prophecies of future events; (5) fantastic imagery, usually involving fearsome animals; and (6) symbolic use of names or numbers. See also canon.

apocrypha From Greek *apokrypha* (*2 Esdras* 12:37–38; 14:45–46), meaning "hidden things"; religious texts, the authority or authenticity of which is questionable. *Apocrypha* can refer to any such texts not in an accepted Old or New Testament canon. Formally, however, the word refers to books in Roman Catholic and Eastern Orthodox Old Testaments that aren't in Protestant Old Testaments, including *Tobit, Judith, Wisdom of Solomon, Ecclesiasticus* (also known as *Wisdom of Sirach*), *Baruch, Letter of Jeremiah, Prayer of Manasseh, 1 and 2 Maccabees, 1 and 2 Esdras,* and additions to the books of Daniel, Esther, and Psalms.

None of these writings appears in the Hebrew Scriptures. Recognizing that Jews had never recognized them as having equal authority, a gathering of Jewish rabbis in AD 90 (later known as the Council of Yavneh [Jamnia]) did not include them in their listing of authoritative texts. In the early 1500s, many Protestants chose to use the Old Testament canon summarized at Yavneh instead of the Roman Catholic Church's; in 1546, the Catholic Council of Trent referred to these books as "deuterocanonical"—that is, part of "a secondary canon." See also Bible; canon; *Esdras; Maccabees.*

Apocryphon of James, The Alternate title for *The Secret Book of James.* See *Secret Book of James.*

Apocryphon of John, The Late-second-century Gnostic writing, found among the Nag Hammadi texts (named for the place of their discovery in Upper [southern] Egypt); claims to have been authored by the apostle John but was clearly written after his death. Like other Gnostic works, *Apocryphon of John* presents an evil deity as the creator of the physical world; Gnostics claimed that this being is the deity of the Old Testament. No early Christian writer considered this document to have any authority for believers or any place among the canonical Scriptures. See also Gnosticism; Nag Hammadi.

Apocryphon of Mark, The Alternate title for *The Secret Gospel of Mark.* See *Secret Gospel of Mark.*

apostle From Greek *apostolos,* meaning "commissioned one" or "the one sent." Eyewitnesses of the resurrected Jesus, commissioned to proclaim and interpret, throughout the world, the meaning of his life and ministry. The original twelve were: Simon, son of John (also known as Peter, Cephas); Andrew, son of John; James, son of Zebedee; John, son of Zebedee; Philip of Bethsaida; Nathanael Bartholomew; Matthew/Levi, son of Alphaeus; James, son of Alphaeus; Judas Thomas Didymus; Simon the Zealot; Judas Iscariot; Judas Thaddeus Lebbaeus (Matt. 10:2–4; Mark 3:16–19; Luke 6:12–16).

After Judas Iscariot betrayed Jesus, Matthias replaced him as the twelfth apostle (Acts 1:21–26). Paul of Tarsus, once known as Saul, later became an apostle through special commission from Jesus (1 Cor. 15:9–10; Gal. 1:1). First-century Christians also considered the testimony of Jesus' physical half-brothers to be apostolic; in Galatians 1:19, for example, Paul referred to "James, the Lord's brother" as one of the apostles. (Note that Roman Catholics do not believe Jesus had half-siblings—they maintain that there are different ways to interpret and understand the biblical passages that lead Protestants to believe otherwise, such as viewing "the Lord's brother" as a reference to one of Joseph's sons from a previous marriage.) According to the traditions preserved by Eusebius and other early historians, nearly all the apostles faced martyrdom for their faith, sealing the truth of their testimony in their own blood. Therefore, when second-century Christians carefully considered what should be understood as canonical or authentic, they concluded that each New Testament writing should be directly connected to an apostle—its veracity testified and upheld to the point of death. See also canon; Pauline Corpus.

apostolic fathers Late-first- and early-second-century Christian teachers and leaders from the first generation after the apostles. The four primary apostolic fathers were Clement of Rome, Ignatius, Polycarp, and Papias.

Important texts from this era include *First Clement, Didache, Epistle of Barnabas, Shepherd of Hermas,* and the fragments of Papias's writings preserved by authors like Eusebius. Some early Christians may have treated these documents as scriptural; however, although their theology was orthodox, they could not be directly connected to specific apostles, so ultimately they were excluded from the canon. See also apostle; *Barnabas, Epistle of; Clement, First;* Clement of Rome; *Didache;* Eusebius of Caesarea; Ignatius of Antioch; Papias of Hierapolis; Polycarp of Smyrna; *Shepherd of Hermas.*

Aramaic Ancient Semitic language, predominant in the Middle East for almost two thousand years, up to the seventh century AD. (Jews and most Arabs are "Semites," descended from Noah's son Shem.) During the twelfth century BC, the Arameans migrated into the Middle East, bringing with them the language that would eventually become Aramaic; the Jewish people used the Aramaic alphabet as the basis for written Hebrew. Ezra 4–7 and Daniel 2–7, in the Hebrew Scriptures, are written in Aramaic; Aramaic was one of the languages Jesus spoke. (See Mark 5:41;

7:34; 14:36; 15:34 for Aramaic words in the Greek New Testament.) See also "companion," Aramaic word for.

Arius of Alexandria Heretical teacher; d. 336; ordained as a pastor in Egypt around 313, Arius began teaching that Jesus is not God but instead is God the Father's first creation. In his words, "There was a time when the Son did not exist." Because the apostles had believed that Jesus is both God (John 10:30–33; 20:28; Rom. 9:5) and man (1 John 4:2; 2 John 1:7), Arius's teachings caused concern and conflict among Christians throughout the Roman empire. This eventually compelled Emperor Constantine to convene the Council of Nicaea in 325; the council condemned the Arian heresy with the Nicene Creed. See also Christology; Constantine the Great; Council of Nicaea.

art, terms and history Given that the title of the novel is *The Da Vinci Code,* named for one of the world's greatest artists, a reader might reasonably expect to discover an accurate and trustworthy source on art and art history. Dan Brown states on page 1 that "all descriptions of artwork, architecture, documents, and secret rituals in this novel are accurate." Such is not the case. The book's art fallacies, many related to Leonardo himself, aren't as numerous as its historical and theological errors. Several are listed throughout this glossary.

One example is noted by Boston University's Dr. Franco Mormando (Associate Professor of Italian; Chair, Department of Romance Languages and Literatures) in the phrase "a Renaissance bedroom with Louis XVI furniture" (*DVC,* 8); this is a contradiction, since "Louis XVI furniture" is later Baroque (seventeenth century) and flamboyant, while "Renaissance" is more austere.

Another (admittedly insignificant) instance of insufficient artistic understanding is found in the term *hand-frescoed walls*—a redundancy, since all fresco is done by hand.

A succinct evaluation of *The Da Vinci Code*'s art credibility is given by Jack Wasserman, retired art professor at Temple University: "Just about everything [Brown] says about Leonardo da Vinci is wrong." (Patrick T. Reardon, "*The Da Vinci Code* . . . Unscrambled." 2/5/04: *Chicago Tribune,* A1.)

Assumption of Moses, The Probably a reference to the now-lost latter chapters of *The Testament of Moses*. See *Testament of Moses*.

astrology From Greek *astrologia,* meaning "sayings about the stars"; study of the positioning of celestial bodies (such as the sun, moon, stars, planets, and comets), as well as the belief that astrological knowledge is useful for understanding and interpreting earthly events. Astrology divides the moon's and planets' paths around the sun into twelve segments; each segment has a name or sign that corresponds with the name of a constellation (a visible collection of stars).

Astrology differs greatly from astronomy, which is the scientific study of individual stars, constellations, and their rotations, orbits, planets, and space. Astrology likewise stands in stark contrast to the biblical perspective, in which cosmic movements are viewed as evidences of the Creator's glory (Ps. 148:1–5; Jer. 31:35; cf. Deut. 4:19). No Christian church advocates belief in the zodiac; its origins are in ancient Babylon and reflect pagan beliefs and teachings about nature. Astrology is often associated with the occult, magic, fortune-telling, and legends that are unrelated to Jesus Christ or his teachings. See also Age of Aquarius; Age of Pisces; zodiac.

Atbash Cipher, The Code, using Hebrew letters, in which each letter is exchanged for an equidistant letter (*DVC,* 303–04). For example, in the English alphabet, a *z* (last letter) would be substituted for an *a* (first letter). A *y* (second from the end) would be substituted for a *b* (second from the beginning). *Atbash* (technically A, T-B, Sh) comes from the Hebrew letters *A*leph, *T*aw, *B*eth, and *S*hin. See also Hebrew.

Athanasius of Alexandria Christian teacher; d. 373; ordained as a deacon in Egypt around 319, Athanasius attended the Council of Nicaea in 325 and soon afterward became the overseer (bishop) of Alexandria. Athanasius spent much of his career confronting Arius's teaching that Jesus is not God.

ATHANASIUS

c. 296—born in Alexandria

c. 308–c. 315—studied under Bishop Alexander

c. 313—brought into Alexander's house, became his secretary

c. 318—wrote *Against the Gentiles* and *On the Incarnation*

c. 319—ordained deacon

c. 325—attended Council of Nicaea

c. 328—elected Bishop of Alexandria

331—appeared before Emperor Constantine

In 367 he wrote a letter (now referred to as the thirty-ninth Festal Letter) to the churches in his area, listing the books meeting the standards set for the New Testament canon (i.e., authoritative writings)—identical to the list that Christians still use today. See also Arius of Alexandria; canon; Christology; church fathers; Constantine the Great; Council of Nicaea.

Attridge, Harold W. Renowned contemporary scholar, author, and editor of books about the New Testament and the Nag Hammadi documents; Dean of Yale University Divinity School. Responding to Dan Brown's claim that Christians did not consider Jesus divine until the fourth century, Attridge said, "People were thinking Jesus was divine in some sense or another from the first century on. . . . [*The Da Vinci Code*] takes facts and gives them a spin that distorts them seriously." See also Christology; Council of Nicaea.

Augustine of Hippo North African theologian and church leader; d. 430. His father seems to have been a pagan; his mother, Monica, was a devout Christian. While a student, Augustine took a concubine to whom he remained faithful for fifteen years; their son, Adeodatus, was born around 373. Soon after, Augustine, beginning an intense search for truth, dismissed Christianity as an unrefined religion and joined the Manichees, a Gnostic-like sect. The Manichaean worldview quickly disillusioned him, but in 384 he moved to Milan to become a professor.

Around the same time he met a group of Christian philosophers that included Ambrose, a church leader. In 386, Augustine underwent a profound conversion; he renounced his career and his concubine, and after Monica's death, he returned to Africa. While visiting the city of Hippo in 391, the church, against his will, ordained him as an elder. When its bishop died, Augustine became his successor. As a leader, Augustine argued that sexuality is not inherently evil, yet at the same time he never

ATHANASIUS
(cont.)

334—refused to attend Council at Caesarea

335—defended himself before Council of Tyre

336-338—endured first exile

c. 344-346—underwent second exile

356-361—suffered third exile, wrote *History of the Arians*

362—returned again to Alexandria

365—forced into fourth exile

367—wrote thirty-ninth Festal Letter

372—wrote *Against Apollinarianism*

373—died peacefully at home

escaped the concept (common to Manichaeism and Platonism) that sexual relations pull the soul downward.

After the Goths sacked Rome in 410, many non-Christians claimed the "Eternal City" had fallen because the Romans had forsaken the ancient gods. In *City of God*, Augustine countered their claims, demonstrating that every human regime—every "City of Mankind"—is bound to fall. Christian worship (especially the Lord's Supper) points us toward the "City of God," the only eternal realm. See also Gnosticism.

Augustus, Caesar Roman emperor; d. AD 14; also known as "Octavian." Born Gaius Octavius Thurinus in 63 BC, Caesar Augustus preserved the outward forms of the Roman republic even as he ruled as emperor for nearly four decades. His mother was the niece of Julius Caesar; in 46 BC, Julius adopted Octavian as his son and heir. After Julius's assassination, Octavian formed an alliance with Julius's two primary rivals (known as "the Second Triumvirate"), and, after then defeating both, knowing that Rome was not yet ready to accept an emperor, Octavian held an election. The people elected Octavian "consul," the highest executive office in the republic. In 27 BC, when Octavian offered to relinquish his power, the senate not only turned down his offer but also gave him additional power and granted him the title "Augustus." By 23 BC, Augustus was emperor ("Caesar") of the Roman territories; his reign marked the beginning of nearly fifty years of civil peace and prosperity, commonly known as the *pax Romana* ("Roman peace"). Jesus Christ was born during this era, and the speed with which Christianity spread throughout the ancient world may be partly attributed to the roads and shipping routes associated with Caesar Augustus.

autograph Term from textual criticism (a type of biblical study) that refers to an original document, as opposed to a copy. Although we do not have the autographs—original writings—of the New Testament documents, copies have been preserved with remarkable precision and accuracy. See also deconstructionism; form criticism; manuscript; papyrus; redaction criticism; textual criticism.

BC Abbreviation for "Before Christ"; a calendar designation intended to represent the years before the birth of Jesus. When calculating the date for Easter in 525, Dionysius Exiguus established that year as the five hundred twenty-fifth since Jesus' birth. His calculations contained enough inaccuracy to be off by about four years; Jesus was probably born in 4 BC, four years before the year designated for his birth. See also AD; BCE; CE.

BCE Abbreviation for "Before the Common Era" or "Before the Christian Era"; a calendar designation intended as an alternative to "BC." See also AD; BC; CE.

Baigent, Michael Coauthor (with Richard Leigh and Henry Lincoln) of *Holy Blood, Holy Grail* (*DVC*, 253). According to the *London Daily Telegraph* ("*Da Vinci Code* author faces plagiarism lawsuit," Hugh Davis, 10/23/05), Dan Brown faces court action from Baigent and Leigh (Lincoln is not involved), who claim that Brown's writing was plagiarized from their research. According to Leigh, "I don't begrudge Brown his success. I have no particular grievance against him, except for the fact that he wrote a pretty bad novel." See *Holy Blood, Holy Grail.*

Baphomet According to Dan Brown, an ancient horned fertility god worshiped by the Knights Templar; this heresy said to be one reason for their persecution by the Church (*DVC*, 316). Contemporary historians assert there is neither real evidence that the Templars worshiped such an idol nor that such a horned god was ever worshiped by ancient cults.

    In pre-Christian Egypt, a cult in the city of Mendes used goats as part of sexual fertility rituals; these bestial acts were known throughout Greek and Roman societies. However, not until 1854, when Eliphas Levi wrote

Transcendental Magic, was the current image of Baphomet created. The horned man-goat was adopted by Anton LaVey in 1966, when he organized the Church of Satan.

The word *Baphomet* may be a slanderous medieval Latin translation of the Arabic word *Muhammad*. In the crusades, Christians commonly misinterpreted or misrepresented Islamic elements so as to unfavorably depict their religion and worship. See also Knights Templar.

Barnabas First-century Christian missionary, native of Cyprus; Joseph Barnabas accompanied the apostle Paul on his first missionary journey. *Barnabas* was a nickname—an Aramaic moniker meaning "son of encouragement" (Acts 4:36). Origen and Clement of Alexandria believed Barnabas wrote the letter known as *Epistle of Barnabas;* this is possible, but by no means certain. See Clement of Alexandria; Origen of Alexandria.

Barnabas, Epistle of Late-first- or early-second-century Christian writing; attributed to Barnabas, an associate of the apostle Paul. A prophecy within it seems to place its date between the destruction of the Jewish temple in AD 70 and the Roman emperor building a pagan temple on its former site in 135: "The ones who destroyed the Temple will themselves rebuild it. That's happening now: During the war, the enemy destroyed the Temple. Yet, in this present time, the enemy's servants will rebuild the Temple."

Clement of Alexandria and Origen quoted from the *Epistle of Barnabas*, which also appears in *Codex Sinaiticus* (in an appendix to the New Testament). However, it was ultimately excluded from the New Testament, probably due to (1) the recognition that, since the Jewish temple was *not* rebuilt "in this present time," it contained a false prophecy and (2) its persistent anti-Jewish tone. See also Barnabas; canon; *Codex Sinaiticus;* temple, Herod's.

Baudelaire, Charles A nineteenth-century French poet, translator, and critic who enjoyed a decadent lifestyle inclusive of drinking and prostitutes. Baudelaire translated the works of Edgar Allan Poe; his own poetry was dark and brooding (*DVC*, 88).

Bauer, Walter Modern German biblical scholar; d. 1960; author of the classic *Orthodoxy and Heresy in Early Christianity* (1934), in which he argued that Jesus' earliest followers didn't distinguish between *orthodoxy* and *heresy*. According to Bauer, in the beginning there were simply varying (and sometimes competing) forms of faith, all of which were regarded as "Christian." In other words, early believers had no specific set of non-negotiable beliefs; this idea supposedly "developed" much later. For several decades this view has remained dominant among theologically liberal scholars; *The Da Vinci Code* presents Bauer's thesis in a fictionalized form. New Testament scholar I. Howard Marshall has provided substantial refutation (e.g., "Orthodoxy and Heresy in Earlier Christianity" in *Themelios*, 9/76 and *New Testament Theology: Many Witnesses, One Gospel* [2004]). See also heresy; orthodoxy.

Benjamin, Tribe of One of the twelve Israelite clans. Apparently basing his statements on Margaret Starbird's writings, Dan Brown has one *Da Vinci Code* character claim that Mary Magdalene was "a powerful woman" and a member of "the house of Benjamin" (*DVC*, 248), further implying that Benjamin was a royal tribe.

In fact, no one knows whether Mary Magdalene was powerful, and there's no evidence she was a Benjaminite. *Magdalene* most likely means "from the village of Magdala," a village on the western side of the Sea of Galilee—many miles from Benjamin's territory on the northern edge of the Dead Sea.

Furthermore, Benjamin was neither royal nor powerful; even during the time of Moses and Joshua, it was a small tribe (Num. 1:36–37; Ps. 68:27) with a small territory (Josh. 18:21–28). Saul, Israel's first king, *was* a Benjaminite; he declared that he was from the weakest tribe (1 Sam. 9:21). After Saul's death, Judah became the nation's sole tribal royalty. Brown's claims that "by marrying into the powerful House of Benjamin, Jesus fused two royal bloodlines" are plainly fictitious (*DVC*, 248). See also Mary Magdalene; Starbird, Margaret.

Bernard of Clairvaux Catholic monk; d. 1153; medieval theologian and leading monk of a monastery in Clairvaux, France. In 1128, Bernard attended a gathering of church leaders in Troyes; wanting to ensure the safety of pilgrims making their way to Jerusalem, Bernard encouraged church leaders to create an order of monks to protect them. This order became known as the Knights Templar. See also Clement V, Pope; Knights Templar.

Bible From Greek *biblia*, "books"; in Christian usage, the collection of writings authoritative for faith and practice. The Protestant Bible consists of thirty-nine books from the Jewish faith (the Old Testament) and twenty-seven Christian writings (the New Testament). The Roman Catholic Old Testament also includes seven "deuterocanonical" books—*Tobit, Judith, 1* and *2 Maccabees, Wisdom of Solomon, Wisdom of Sirach* (*Ecclesiasticus*), and *Baruch* (with *Letter of Jeremiah*)—plus additions to Daniel (*Susanna, Bel and the Dragon*) and Esther. The Eastern Orthodox Old Testament contains several writings not found in Catholic or Protestant Bibles—*Esdras, Prayer of Manasseh, Psalm 151, Odes, 3* and *4 Maccabees,* and *Psalms of Solomon.*

These differences should *not* obscure the overwhelming degree of agreement on the Bible's content: There are sixty-six books to which Catholic, Orthodox, and Protestant Christians share a common commitment, writings that provide believers with an awe-inspiring record of God's nature and character. Vigorously attacked, the Bible has withstood the most overwhelming scrutiny, being repeatedly found historically reliable. In contrast to the world's other religions, which depict humanity attempting to reach God, the scriptural account is one of a God who reaches down to humanity.

The penning of these works spans roughly fifteen hundred years through more than forty authors, yet the Old and New Testament books exhibit remarkable unity. The Old Testament authors allude to a new "covenant" (agreement or contract) that was later revealed through Jesus Christ (Jer. 31:31–34); the New Testament confirms the full authenticity and dependability of the Old (John 10:35; 2 Tim. 3:14–16) *and* asserts its own equal authority (e.g., 1 Timothy 5:18 quotes Luke 10:7 as Scripture; see also 2 Peter 3:15–16). See apocrypha; canon; *Esdras;* Muratorian Fragment.

Bibliothèque Nationale de France National Library of France, in Paris, where in 1967, Pierre Plantard placed the forged and fraudulent *Les Dossiers Secrets.* These are the bases for Dan Brown's belief that the Priory of Sion has long existed and has included such well-known figures as

Leonardo da Vinci and Isaac Newton. See *Dossiers Secrets, Les;* Plantard, Pierre; Priory of Sion.

Black Madonna A term that may apply to (A) a painting or sculpture that has darkened over time from candle-smoke or dirt, or a black statue often thought to be the Virgin Mary, or (B) a painting or sculpture originally created with dark skin. There are many interpretations as to the origins and meanings of the dark-skinned madonnas, but one of interest for *Da Vinci Code* readers comes from southern France. A legend says that Mary Magdalene traveled there with Mary, the mother of James and John, the Virgin Mary, and their servant girl, Sarah. Seventeen centuries later—in 1686—the young girl Sarah was named the patron saint of the European Gypsies and was said to be the mother of the Black Madonna. See Notre-Dame-de-la-Mer.

blade According to Dan Brown, the symbol of masculinity (*DVC,* 237); borrowed heavily from Riane Eisler's *Chalice and the Blade.* Dipping a blade into a chalice is a Wiccan ritual.

Blomberg, Craig L. Contemporary biblical scholar at Denver Seminary; recognized New Testament authority. Blomberg's *Historical Reliability of the Gospels* (1987) demonstrates that the four canonicals—Matthew, Mark, Luke, and John—provide accurate descriptions of the life, ministry, and teachings of Jesus Christ. See also canon; Gospels, canonical.

Boaz and Jachin Masonic pillars. At the Rosslyn Chapel near Edinburgh, Scotland, *The Da Vinci Code*'s Robert Langdon calls them "the most duplicated architectural structures in history" (435–36), a claim difficult to substantiate. He further states that they are the "exact replicas" of two pillars scripturally referenced (1 Kings 7:15–22; 2 Kings 25:16–17; 2 Chron. 3:15–17; 4:12–13; Jer 52:21–23), of which the precise specifications and intricacies are simply not known—certainly there isn't enough information to ascertain what could be  "exact replicas." In biblical times, the names of the two columns seem to have stood for certain declarations about God. The *Jachin* (*Jakin*) pillar appears to have meant, "Yahweh will establish [*yakin* or *Jachin*] thy throne forever." The *Boaz* pillar is believed to have represented "In Yahweh is the king's strength," specifically affirming the Hebrew (Old Testament) God. See also Rosslyn Chapel.

Bock, Darrell L. Author of *Breaking the Da Vinci Code.*

Bois de Boulogne Parisian park designed by landscape architect Jean-Charles Alphand, consisting of promenades, lakes, and playgrounds, modeled after London's parks. Filled with rowers, runners, and picnickers by day; frequented by prostitutes by night (*DVC*, 157).

Botticelli, Sandro d. 1510; said by Dan Brown to have been a Grand Master of the Priory of Sion (as according to *Les Dossiers Secrets*); better known—and more historically founded—as one of Florence's great Renaissance artists. Brown's inclusion of Botticelli among his esoteric pantheon likely stems from the quality of distinct feminine spirituality in such paintings as *Birth of Venus* and *Primavera.* If there is any accuracy in *any* portion of the Priory conspiracy, it is offset by Botticelli, near the end of his life, having been deeply impacted by the fiery reformist preacher Girolamo Savonarola. See also *Les Dossiers Secrets;* Plantard, Pierre; Renaissance.

Breaking the Da Vinci Code *Answers to the Questions Everyone is Asking* (DVD); Grizzly Adams Productions, Inc; David W. Balsiger, Producer.

Brown, Dan Author of *The Da Vinci Code,* born in 1964, in Exeter, New Hampshire. His mother, a professional musician, played the organ and specialized in sacred music; as a boy Brown attended Sunday school, sang in the choir, and went to

DAN BROWN

1964—born (Exeter, New Hampshire)

1982—graduated from Phillips Exeter Academy

1985—studied art history at University of Seville

1986—graduated from Amherst College

1987-1990—formed record company, self-published cassette and CD

1991—moved to Hollywood, pursued career as pianist/ songwriter; taught Spanish classes at prep school; met and later married Blythe Newlon

1993-94—released CDs *Dan Brown* and *Angels & Demons*

1993—moved back to New Hampshire; became English teacher at Phillips Exeter

1994—Vacationing in Tahiti, reading a popular suspense novel, was struck by the inspiration to write and do it better; began *Digital Fortress*

summer church camp. He was educated at Phillips Exeter Academy—where his Presidential Award-winning father taught mathematics—and Amherst College, where he graduated in 1986; he speaks of his formative years as a consistently blended interplay between the realms of faith and science. He claims to be a "Christian," a term he says everyone defines in accordance with personal beliefs.

After studying abroad and then living on the West Coast, Brown taught English at Exeter before turning to full-time writing. His *Digital Fortress* (a novel dealing with cryptology), *Deception Point,* and *Angels & Demons* were each published before *The Da Vinci Code,* which exploded into a record-setting bestseller after Doubleday initially expected to print a few thousand copies. Despite its sales of more than 40 million units, *Da Vinci Code* has been roundly and severely criticized for both factual inaccuracies and literary flaws.

Bruce, Frederick F. Biblical scholar; d. 1990; esteemed New Testament expert; Rylands Professor of Biblical Criticism and Exegesis at the University of Manchester. His books *The New Testament Documents: Are They Reliable?* (1982) and *The Canon of Scripture* (1990) provide historical evidence that soundly disproves many *Da Vinci Code* claims. See also canon.

Burstein, Dan Editor of *Secret of the Code: The Unauthorized Guide to the Mysteries Behind The Da Vinci Code;* includes chapters written by a broad group, with variety ranging from scholars to "alternative history buffs," including Karen King, Elaine Pagels, Margaret Starbird, and Lynn Picknett.

DAN BROWN
(cont.)

1994—Coauthored *187 Men to Avoid: A Guide for the Romantically Frustrated Woman* (humor, under pseudonym "Danielle Brown," with Blythe)

1996—Stopped teaching to become full-time writer

1998—*Digital Fortress* published; co-authored *The Bald Book* (humor)

2000—*Angels & Demons* published

2001—*Deception Point* published

2003—*The Da Vinci Code* published

2004—All four novels concurrently on *New York Times* Best-Seller list

2004—Donated $2.2 million to Phillips Exeter, with siblings, in honor of their father, Richard G. Brown

2005—Made *Time* magazine's "100 Most Influential People of the Year"

CE Abbreviation for "Common Era" or "Christian Era"; a calendar designation intended as an alternative to AD. See also AD; BC; BCE.

caducei Plural of *caduceus,* ancient wand or staff associated with Greek mythology and, specifically, the god Hermes. Occasionally confused with the symbolic staff of the medical profession (*DVC,* 23).

canon From Greek *kanon,* "measuring stick." Religious texts authoritative for members of a given religion (*DVC,* 231–32).

OLD TESTAMENT CANON: In AD 90, Jewish rabbis at the Council of Yavneh (also known as Jamnia) formally *recognized* (rather than *established*) thirty-nine books as authoritative Scripture for the Jewish faith—the texts the Jewish people had for centuries already received as authoritative. These books are the same that appear in Protestant Bibles today. The Old Testament canons of the Roman Catholic and Eastern Orthodox Churches include several books (*deuterocanonical,* or *apocryphal*) that do not appear in the Jewish canon. See also apocrypha; Bible; Marcion of Sinope.

NEW TESTAMENT CANON: According to Dan Brown, the New Testament canon did not emerge until the fourth century, when books were compiled and edited by men who possessed "a political agenda . . . to solidify their own power base" (*DVC,* 234). It is true that the New Testament underwent a compilation process; however, most of it was established before the second century—twenty of the twenty-seven books were accepted as part of the Christian canon from the very beginning. This list included the four gospels, Acts, the thirteen letters of Paul, 1 Peter, and 1 John. Even if the New Testament had included only these writings, every essential doctrine of the Christian faith would remain intact.

In the second century, when Marcion of Sinope questioned the authority of some of these writings, a threefold consensus among church leaders emerged about whether a book should be accepted as canonical or authentic:

(1) Because the apostles were the eyewitnesses of Jesus' resurrection, the writing had to be directly connected to an apostle.
(2) The writing had to be "orthodox"; that is, it could not contradict Old Testament or apostolic teachings.
(3) The writing had to be accepted in churches throughout the known world; in other words, it could not be accepted only by one group of believers.

These requirements specifically prevented canon manipulation by any single group. Disagreements did continue concerning several books, including Hebrews, James, 2 Peter, 2 and 3 John, Jude, Revelation, *Didache, Epistle of Barnabas, Shepherd of Hermas, Diatessaron, Gospel of the Hebrews, Acts of Paul,* and *Apocalypse of Peter.* Hebrews, James, 2 Peter, 2 and 3 John, Jude, and Revelation were recognized as meeting the threefold test of canonicity (see first chart below).

In 367, the Festal Letter of Athanasius listed as an authoritative canon the same twenty-seven books that appear in modern New Testaments. See also *Acts of Paul; Apocalypse of Peter;* apocrypha; Athanasius of Alexandria; Bible; Bruce, Frederick F.; *Diatessaron; Didache; Epistle of Barnabas;* Eusebius of Caesarea; *Gospel of the Hebrews;* Marcion of Sinope; Muratorian Fragment; orthodoxy; *Shepherd of Hermas.*

For understanding of Old and New Testament formation, three charts follow:

- Why Writings Were Included In or Excluded From the Bible
- New Testament and Early Church Writings: Comparisons From the First Four Centuries
- The Final Result: Comparisons of Bibles (Protestant, Roman Catholic, Eastern Orthodox, Russian Orthodox)

WHY WRITINGS WERE INCLUDED IN OR EXCLUDED FROM THE BIBLE
(OLD TESTAMENT)

Writing	Reason for Acceptance As Authoritative	Reason for Exclusion
Torah ("Law"): Genesis, Exodus, Leviticus, Numbers, Deuteronomy	From the time of Moses, Israel accepted God's self-revelation to Moses through the Torah as the authoritative standard for their lives. Further writings could be accepted as authoritative only if they conformed to the Torah.	
Nevi'im (Prophets): Joshua, Judges, Samuel (1 and 2), Kings (1 and 2), Isaiah, Jeremiah, Ezekiel, Minor Prophets (Hosea, Joel, Amos, Obadiah, Jonah, Micah, Nahum, Habakkuk, Zephaniah, Haggai, Zechariah, Malachi)	At least as early as the intertestamental period (c. 400–4 BC), these writings were recognized as authoritative prophetic utterances conforming to God's self-revelation in the Torah. During this time, the Jewish people came to understand that divine prophecies had ceased (for whatever length of time) after these books were written. The deuterocanonical *1 Maccabees* says (9:27), "There was great distress in Israel, such as had not occurred since the time that *the prophets ceased to appear.*"	

Writing	Reason for Acceptance As Authoritative	Reason for Exclusion
Kethubim (Writings): Psalms, Proverbs, Job, Song of Songs, Ruth, Lamentations, Ecclesiastes, Esther, Daniel, Ezra-Nehemiah, Chronicles (1 and 2)	In addition to conforming to the Torah's teachings, these Hebrew documents had important functions in corporate worship and personal devotion. They complete the "twenty-four books" that—according to the author of *2 Esdras* (14:45–46)—the Jews accepted as universally authoritative. (The Jews consider their Bible to have twenty-four books, rather than the Protestant Old Testament thirty-nine, because they count the twelve minor prophets as a single book, and they group together 1 and 2 Samuel, 1 and 2 Kings, 1 and 2 Chronicles, and Ezra-Nehemiah.)	
Tobit, Judith, additions to Esther, *1* and *2 Maccabees, Wisdom of Solomon, Wisdom of Sirach (Ecclesiasticus), Baruch,* additions to Daniel (*Susanna, Bel and the Dragon*)		Accepted by Roman Catholic and Eastern Orthodox Churches, but excluded by Jews and Protestants for the following reasons: (1) These apocryphal (or deuterocanonical) books, never part of the Hebrew Bible, were later additions written in Greek. (2) They stand outside the twenty-four books recognized at least as early as the late-first century AD as God's authoritative self-revelation to the Jewish people.

Writing	Reason for Acceptance As Authoritative	Reason for Exclusion
1 Esdras (called *2 Esdras* in the Russian Orthodox Church), *Prayer of Manasseh, Psalm 151, 3* and *4 Maccabees*		Accepted by the Eastern Orthodox, but excluded by Jews and Protestants for the same reasons as with other apocryphal books. The Roman Catholic Church excludes them primarily because they were never widely accepted or used in the Western half of the Roman empire.
2 Esdras (called *3 Esdras* in the Russian Orthodox Church)		Accepted by the Russian Orthodox (Slavonic) and Ethiopian Orthodox Churches. Other Christians exclude *2 Esdras* largely because it was written after the time of Jesus Christ and because it wasn't universally recognized among Christians.

WHY WRITINGS WERE INCLUDED IN OR EXCLUDED FROM THE BIBLE (NEW TESTAMENT)

Writing	Reason for Acceptance As Authoritative	Reason for Exclusion
Matthew	One of Jesus' first followers, Matthew was an eyewitness of his life and ministry.	
Mark	John Mark served as the apostle Peter's translator; as such, the words of Mark's gospel reflect Peter's eyewitness testimony.	

Writing	Reason for Acceptance As Authoritative	Reason for Exclusion
Luke and Acts	Luke was an associate of Paul (Col. 4:14; 2 Tim. 4:11; Philem. 24), an apostle specially commissioned by Christ.	
John, 1, 2, and 3 John, Revelation	One of Jesus' first followers, John was an eyewitness of his life and ministry.	
Romans, 1 and 2 Corinthians, Galatians, Ephesians, Philippians, Colossians, 1 and 2 Thessalonians, 1 and 2 Timothy, Titus, Philemon	Paul was an eyewitness of the resurrected Jesus, who personally commissioned him as an apostle (Acts 9:1–17; 1 Cor. 15:8–10; Gal. 1:13–16).	
Hebrews	Although initially disputed, Hebrews was accepted into the canon because of its connection (through Timothy) to the apostle Paul (13:23).	
James	Because James was Jesus' physical half-brother, his testimony to Jesus was viewed as apostolic and authoritative (Gal. 1:19).	
1 and 2 Peter	One of Christ's first followers, Simon Peter was an eyewitness of his life and ministry.	
Jude	Jude seems also to have been a physical half-brother of Jesus. As such, his testimony—like that of James—was viewed as apostolic and authoritative (See Gal. 1:19).	

Writing	Reason for Acceptance As Authoritative	Reason for Exclusion
Didache		Although completely orthodox and in agreement with the canonical New Testament, *Didache* was eventually excluded from the canon, possibly because it could not be clearly connected to an apostle.
The Epistle of Barnabas		Appears in *Codex Sinaiticus* in an appendix to the New Testament, but was ultimately excluded from the New Testament, probably because it contains a false prophecy and because of its anti-Jewish tone.
Shepherd of Hermas		Excluded primarily because it could not be connected to an eyewitness of Jesus; probably written around 150 by the brother of Pius, bishop of Rome.
Diatessaron		Harmonized (and edited) version of the canonical Gospels; probably excluded because it didn't provide any new material.
The Gospel of the Hebrews		Has been lost; may have been an early version of the canonical gospel of Matthew.

Writing	Reason for Acceptance As Authoritative	Reason for Exclusion
The Acts of Paul		Excluded because it didn't represent historical testimony. A church leader admitted around 160 that he'd written this novel "out of respect for Paul."
The Apocalypse of Peter		Rejected (although completely orthodox) because Peter didn't write it. (Authored around 135, long after his death.)

NEW TESTAMENT AND EARLY CHURCH WRITINGS:
COMPARISONS FROM THE FIRST FOUR CENTURIES

First Century

Gnostic Writings (non-canonical)	Unorthodox Writings (non-canonical)	Christian Writings (non-canonical)	Christian Writings (canonical)
		*1 Clement *Didache	Galatians (49), James (49?), Matthew (50–70), 1 Thessalonians (51), 2 Thessalonians (52), 1 Corinthians (55), 2 Corinthians (57), Romans (58), 1 Peter (60s?), Hebrews (60s?), Philippians (61), Ephesians/Colossians/Philemon (62), 2 Peter (65), Mark (65), Jude (65–70?), Luke-Acts (65–70), 1 Timothy (66), 2 Timothy, Titus (67), Revelation (late 60s or mid-90s), John & 1, 2, 3 John (90s)

* = Writings ultimately excluded from the canon that some early Christians had considered to be canonical

Second Century

Gnostic Writings (non-canonical)	Unorthodox Writings (non-canonical)	Christian Writings (non-canonical)	Christian Writings (canonical)
Gospel of Thomas (NH), *Secret Book of James* (NH), *Dialogue of the Savior* (NH), *Gospel of Basilides, Gospel of Truth* (NH), *Apocryphon of John* (NH), *Gospel of Judas, Gospel of Eve, Acts of Thomas* (NH)	*Gospel of the Ebionites, Gospel of Peter*	**Epistle of Barnabas, *Apocalypse of Peter, Gospel of Matthias, Gospel of the Egyptians, Shepherd of Hermas, *Diatessaron, Infancy Gospel of Thomas, Infancy Gospel of James, Acts of John, Acts of Paul, Acts of Peter*	

Third Century

Vision of the Savior, Gospel of Mary (NH), *Gospel of Philip* (NH), *Coptic Gospel of the Egyptians* (NH), *Coptic Apocalypse of Peter* (NH)		*Acts of Andrew*	

Fourth Century

Coptic Apocalypse of Paul (NH)		*Gospel of Nicodemus, Apocalypse of Paul*	

* = Writings ultimately excluded from the canon that some early Christians had considered to be canonical

NH = Writings found at Nag Hammadi

THE FINAL RESULT: COMPARISONS OF BIBLES

Protestant Canon	Roman Catholic Canon	Eastern Orthodox Canon	Russian Orthodox Canon
The sixty-six books listed above under "Why Writings Were Included In or Excluded From the Bible" (second column)	The sixty-six, plus *Tobit, Judith, Wisdom of Solomon, Wisdom of Sirach* (*Ecclesiasticus*)*, Baruch, 1* and *2 Maccabees,* additions to Daniel and Esther	The sixty-six, plus *1 Esdras, Tobit, Judith, Psalm 151, Wisdom of Solomon, Wisdom of Sirach* (*Ecclesiasticus*)*, Baruch, Odes* (with *Prayer of Manasseh*)*, 1, 2, 3,* and *4 Maccabees,* additions to Daniel and Esther	The sixty-six, plus *1* and *2 Esdras, Tobit, Judith, Psalm 151, Wisdom of Solomon, Wisdom of Sirach* (*Ecclesiasticus*)*, Baruch, Prayer of Manasseh, 1, 2, 3,* and *4 Maccabees,* additions to Daniel and Esther

Caravaggio Italian painter; d. 1610; his artwork is referenced in *The Da Vinci Code*'s opening pages (3, 32).

Carpocratians, The Second-century Gnostics characterized by sexual promiscuity. Knowledge of them comes from a dubious letter, allegedly written by Clement of Alexandria to "Theodore," stating that the Carpocratians had corrupted a second version of Mark's gospel, known as *The Secret Gospel of Mark,* which included overtones of homosexual acts between Jesus and a young man. However, apparently the letter is a hoax forged by Dr. Morton Smith, professor of ancient history at Columbia University, which he then "discovered" in 1958, in the Mar Saba library near Jerusalem. No one except Dr. Smith has seen the alleged letter, nor is anyone allowed to examine it. See also Gnosticism; *Secret Gospel of Mark;* Smith, Morton.

Castel Gandolfo See *Specula Vaticana.*

Castigo corpus meum A self-flagellation practice, included in *The Da Vinci Code* (14) as connected with Opus Dei, based in part on 1 Corinthians 9:27, from the Latin (Vulgate) translation: "I discipline my body and bring it into subjection" (NKJV); "I beat my body and make it my slave" (NIV).

Cathari From Greek *katharoi*, "pure ones"; group that arose within the Catholic Church in the tenth century, living simply, speaking out against the medieval clergy's corruption, and promoting a Gnostic view of God and of the world. The Cathari believed in two deities, one evil and one good: the evil ("the Demiurge") was the creator of the physical world, worshiped by the Jewish people; the good had created the spiritual world and then Christ to provide a path of escape from the physical world. (Christ supposedly was a phantom, not God-incarnate.) Several pseudo-historical sources, including *Holy Blood, Holy Grail*, have insinuated that a nineteenth-century priest named Bérenger Saunière found evidence in his church at Rennes-Le-Château that the Cathari were the keepers of the Holy Grail; no objective evidence has ever been advanced to support this speculation. See also Albigensian Crusade; Cathar treasure; Gnosticism; *Holy Blood, Holy Grail*; Holy Grail; Saunière, Bérenger.

Cathar treasure Pseudo-historical theory that the Cathari (a Gnostic-type group, circa tenth through thirteenth centuries) possessed a significant artifact or secret hidden during the Albigensian Crusade. *Holy Blood, Holy Grail* alleges that the Cathari were wealthy and possessed secret evidence that Jesus had children with Mary Magdalene. (*The Da Vinci Code* presents this as historical fact.) Despite the theory's popularity, though, there is no objective historical data to support it. Contemporary accounts say the Cathari lived simply and did not possess great wealth. Furthermore, they didn't even believe Jesus was human—they viewed him as a bodiless spiritual being—so it's highly unlikely they were the keepers of evidence that Jesus had children. See Albigensian Crusade; Cathari; Gnosticism; *Holy Blood, Holy Grail*; Mary Magdalene; Saunière, Bérenger.

celibacy See marriage, Jewish.

chalice Mythologically, refers to a vessel that Jesus is believed to have used at the Last Supper; generally, the word can also refer to the cup used for the Roman Catholic Eucharist. In the Middle Ages, various evolving legends labeled the Last Supper chalice as the elusive "Holy Grail." Dan Brown reinterprets the chalice (or grail) to refer to the womb of Mary Magdalene and, by extension, to Mary herself. Lacking historical evidence, Brown claims that Mary carried Jesus' offspring (*DVC*, 162, 237). See also Holy Grail.

Chartres Cathedral Located in Chartres (*DVC,* 7), fifty-five miles south-west of Paris; renowned in the eleventh century as a center of learning. A popular pilgrimage site, Chartres is best known for its Gothic cathedral, Notre Dame de Chartres. In his fine book *Mont-Saint-Michel and Chartres,* American historian Henry Adams sought to explain the power of the "age of faith" evident in two great medieval French buildings. The cathedral in Chartres, perhaps the most beautiful in all France, ever awes visitors with its soaring 120-foot interior, held in place by spider-like flying buttresses supporting its walls and making possible its unrivaled stained-glass windows, considered by many the finest ever made. The cathedral is noted for its ten thousand sculptures—two thousand of them in the entry portals—and 174 stained-glass windows, containing 3,884 figures. Adams said the cathedral's south tower, reaching 304 feet into the sky, is "the most perfect piece of architecture in the world."

Chauvel, Marie Though a woman by this name is the grandmother of *The Da Vinci Code*'s Sophie Neveu, the historical Marie Chauvel de Chauvigny was a "bishop" in the *Église Gnostique Apostolic*—the French Gnostic Church of the Apostles. The church was founded by Jules Doinel, who claimed to be the successor to a series of bishops traced through the medieval Albigensians to the ancient apostolic church.

chevron Military symbol; a set of stripes meeting at an angle on the uniform sleeve (generally of a non-commissioned officer), indicating rank or service. *The Da Vinci Code* sees the chevron representing either the male (inverted-V-formation stripes) or the female (V-formation stripes) genitalia (*DVC,* 237).

Christ From Greek *Christos,* "anointed one." Greek translation of the Hebrew *Moshiakh* ("Messiah"). See Christology; Messiah.

Christmas See December 25.

Christianity as "borrowed" One significant *Da Vinci Code* statement pertains to Dan Brown's perception of the relationship between Christianity and paganism: "By fusing pagan symbols, dates, and rituals into the growing Christian tradition, [Constantine] created a kind of hybrid religion that was acceptable to both parties. . . . The vestiges of pagan religion in Christian symbology are undeniable. . . . Virtually all the elements of the Catholic ritual . . . were taken directly from earlier pagan mystery religions. . . . Nothing in Christianity is original" (*DVC*, 232). These statements are both true and false.

The false: Christianity is, at its core, antithetical to every other world religion, all of which can be depicted as *humankind* striving to reach God or to experience some form of inner peace. Christianity is the account of *God* reaching out to humanity, granting people the opportunity to experience purpose and peace through his offer of salvation. Christianity is summarized as God, in light of humanity's inability to reach him, taking the initiative, bridging the gap; a person is redeemed not by what he or she can do but by what God has already done. In contrast to Brown's claim that "nothing in Christianity is original," Christianity represents a unique and original understanding of the spiritual realm.

The true: The Christian faith does have symbols and words that have come from pagan, pre-Christian sources. However, this is not because early Christianity was so impoverished as to be unable to create its own symbols; rather, its early growth was so rapid that it tended to "retool" already-existing cultural concepts and give them new meaning. For example:

- Baptism was a pre-Christian concept that Christianity redefined as an event whereby a believer identifies first with Jesus' death (going under the water) and then with his resurrection (coming up out of the water).
- The Greek term *agapé* was a pre-Christian word that in Paul's writings takes on new content, depicting God's spectacular love for humanity.
- Easter, once a pagan holiday and even a pagan term (*Eostre*), is now viewed by billions worldwide as the primary celebration of the resurrection of Jesus Christ.
- Brown suggests that Sunday was originally for the pagan "sun god" and that unsuspecting Christians now worship on that day by default (*DVC*, 233). Actually, believers worship weekly on the day that commemorates the resurrection of Christ, which affirms Jesus' authority over life itself—and every other entity—on *all* the days of the week. Also, contrary to *The Da Vinci Code,* Sunday worship began over two hundred years before Constantine supposedly initiated the change from

Saturday (the Jewish Sabbath) to Sunday.

Brown seems to see the Christian "taking" of the Christmas date (December 25) for the celebration of Jesus' birth as a sort of sinister or covert replacement of a pagan holiday. We don't know the actual date of Christ's birth; the point is, Christianity has adapted well to preceding cultural constructs, often by adopting and redefining them.

The compelling, magnetic nature of Jesus' message has proven to be so prevailing that the movement has grown from 120 in a small room (Acts 1:15) to over two billion, with about one-third of the earth's population identifying with the name of Jesus Christ. The issue is less about the church "borrowing" pagan concepts and more about authentic Christianity's magnificent capacity to adapt and adopt *without* losing the core of its Christocentric message. See also Constantine the Great; Council of Nicaea; December 25; Sabbath; *Sol Invictus.*

Christology Subfield of theology; the study of Jesus Christ. In *The Da Vinci Code,* Dan Brown claims fourth-century-Emperor Constantine had the New Testament books embellished to make Jesus appear "godlike." However, throughout the New Testament books (which were completed in the *first* century), the followers of Jesus clearly affirmed that he is not only the Messiah but also fully human (John 1:14; 1 John 4:1–6) and fully God (John 1:1; 8:58 [cf. Ex. 3:14]; 10:30–33; 20:28; Rom. 9:5; Phil. 2:5–6; Heb. 1:8). In the late-first and second centuries, the Gnostics challenged this orthodox understanding, teaching that Jesus only *seemed* human. This belief (known as *Docetism,* from the Greek word *to seem*) was soundly rejected by orthodox believers.

When the Arians later denied Christ's full deity, the Council of Nicaea (325) reaffirmed apostolic teaching, concluding that Jesus was "begotten of the Father before all ages, Light from Light, True God from True God." In what Brown contends was a "close vote" (*DVC,* 233), the orthodox view (that Jesus was both divine and human) passed 316 to 2, overwhelmingly affirming the doctrine Christians had believed (and died for) for several centuries.

In the fifth century, the Monophysites emphasized Jesus' divine nature to a degree that they neglected his humanity. In response, the Council of Chalcedon (451) again echoed apostolic teaching, declaring that Jesus was "perfect in deity and also perfect in humanity; truly God and truly human."

CHART OF CHRISTOLOGICAL ERRORS
by Jim Garlow, edited by Timothy Paul Jones

Errors Denying the Human Element

Docetism (70-170)	Apollinarianism (4th century)
Jesus did not possess a human body. His humanity was an illusion. *Jesus was wholly divine but not human.*	Jesus did not possess a human mind. Its place was taken by logos (divine reason). *Jesus was divine but had an incomplete human nature.*

Errors Denying the Divine Element

Ebionism (70-325)	Arianism (3rd & 4th century)
Jesus received God's Spirit at his baptism as an endowment for his Messianic work. *Jesus was a Spirit-endowed human.*	Jesus was lower than God but higher than man, so he should be viewed as the first of God's creation. *Jesus was a demi-god or semi-divine.*
Adoptionism (8th century) By the descent of the Holy Spirit upon him, Jesus was adopted into the Godhead. *Jesus is the man who became God.*	**Socinianism (6th century)** In early forms, Christ received the Spirit by baptism; in later forms, he was a man of exceptional power. *Jesus was a divinized man.*

Errors Denying the Unity of the Person (embracing two natures)

Nestorianism (4th century)	Eutychianism (5th century)
(Also known as Hyper-Dyophysitism) Jesus was human and divine, but these natures were completely separate. *Jesus had two natures that constituted two persons.*	The elements of Jesus' humanity and divinity mixed together to form a third nature. *Jesus was a mingling of two natures that made a third.*
Monophysitism (6th century) The elements of Jesus' humanity and divinity mixed together to form a single, mingled nature. *In Jesus, two natures became one nature.*	**Monotheletism (7th century)** Christ possessed two natures—one human and one divine—but he possessed only a divine will. *Jesus' humanity was deficient because it lacked a truly human will.*

Errors Denying the Distinctions in the Godhead

Modalistic Monarchianism or Sabellianism (3rd century)	Dynamic Monarchianism (3rd century)
There is one God, and the Father, Son, and Holy Spirit are simply different expressions of one divine person.	Jesus was not in his nature truly God.
Jesus and the Father are not distinct in any way.	*God existed in Jesus the way he exists in all of us.*

Patripassianism (3rd century)

God the Father became incarnate, suffered and died.

God the Father became his own Son.

The eighth century saw the emergence of the Adoptionist heresy, that Jesus was a human being who became divine at baptism. John's gospel, written by an immediate eyewitness, had affirmed that Jesus was divine from the beginning (1:1; 8:58), so the church rejected this belief as well. See also Adoptionism; Arius of Alexandria; Constantine the Great; Council of Nicaea; Docetism; Gnosticism; Separationist Christology.

church fathers Prominent, influential Christian teachers and scholars from the late-first century through the eighth century. The term *church fathers* includes four groups:

- *apostolic fathers:* church leaders in the first generation after the apostles. Most influential: Clement of Rome, Ignatius of Antioch, Polycarp of Smyrna, and Papias of Hierapolis.
- *Greek fathers:* leading Christian scholars whose native language was Greek and who wrote between the second and the eighth centuries: e.g., Irenaeus of Lyons, Clement of Alexandria, and Athanasius of Alexandria.
- *Latin fathers:* Western Christian figures who wrote primarily in Latin; among them are Tertullian of Carthage, Augustine of Hippo, and Jerome.
- *desert fathers:* Christian leaders who wrote very little but had widespread influence. The greatest were Anthony and Pachomius.

The church fathers' era ended in the late-eighth century with John of Damascus. See also apostle; apostolic fathers; Athanasius of Alexandria;

Augustine of Hippo; *Clement, First;* Clement of Alexandria; Clement of Rome; Ignatius of Antioch; Irenaeus of Lyons; Jerome; Papias of Hierapolis; Polycarp of Smyrna; Tertullian of Carthage.

cilice The original meaning of *cilice* describes a rough animal-hair shirt, like one John the Baptist may have worn (Matt. 3:4). In modern times it may also refer to a barbed or spiked chain worn on the thigh as a deterrent to immoral or inappropriate sexual desires (*DVC,* 12).

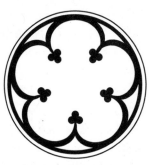

cinquefoil A wild, bushy plant (five-fingered weed) with five-petaled flowers, allegedly (especially in neo-pagan circles) possessing medicinal powers. In artistic work, a *cinquefoil* is a circular carving with five arcs on the circumference. See Rose as symbol.

circle Geometrical symbol; a closed-plane curve with all points equidistant from the center. Serves in various religious traditions as a symbol for perfection, timelessness, and sometimes even magical power: the stones at Stonehenge are arranged in a circle, American Indians celebrated "sacred circles," Zen disciples consider the circle a sign for the absolute, and New Age groups (such as the "Circle Sanctuary" and "Crimson Circle") call people to return to nature and embrace pagan practices in accord with Wiccan precepts. See also *Vitruvian Man.*

clef de voûte French phrase meaning "keystone" (*DVC,* 9, 13), referring to the final stone placed at the crest of an arch (e.g., those providing entryways to Gothic cathedrals), locking it firmly and providing support for the walls and ceiling. Dan Brown alleges that this breakthrough was among the "best-kept secrets of the early Masonic brotherhood" (*DVC,* 203), though it was widely used by architects long before the Masons appeared. Symbolically, *keystone* means "final factor," bringing resolution to a task or inquiry.

Clement V, Pope Roman Catholic pope (r. 1305–1314); first to reign from France. To avoid political difficulties in Rome, Clement V settled at a monastery in Avignon, near France's southern border. According to Dan Brown, "In concert with France's King Philip IV, [Clement V] devised an ingeniously planned sting operation to quash the Templars and seize their treasure. . . . Countless Knights were captured, tortured mercilessly, then burned at the stake as heretics. . . . Many of them were burned at the stake and tossed unceremoniously into the Tiber River" (*DVC*, 159–60, 338). *The Da Vinci Code* maintains that the desired "treasure" was proof that Jesus and Mary Magdalene had been married.

Several serious problems plague *DVC*'s summary. Pope Clement V, weak and sickly, was manipulated by Philip's lust for Templar wealth. *Philip* devised the plan to destroy the Knights, and he was unconcerned with any supposed proof about Jesus and Mary. Second, fewer than 150 Knights were burned—inexcusable, but far from the "countless" burnings Brown posits. Finally, in one of *DVC*'s more absurd errors, none of the bodies could have been "tossed . . . into the Tiber River." The Tiber is in Rome; the trials and executions of the Knights Templar—like the headquarters of Clement V—were in France. See also Knights Templar; Philip IV, King.

Clement, First Late-first-century Christian writing; also known as *The First Epistle/Letter of Clement.* Probably written by Clement of Rome (who early Christians held in high honor), *1 Clement* is a letter to the church at Corinth, which had removed several leaders from their positions. Because none had committed any moral offenses, Clement believed the church's actions were unwarranted. Although some early Christians used *1 Clement* alongside the books now found in the New Testament, it was never considered part of the canon. See also canon; Clement of Rome.

Clement of Alexandria Church leader; d. c. 216; author of writings—*Protrepticus* ("Encouragement"), *Paedagogus* ("Instructor"), and *Stromata* ("Miscellanies")—that attempted to explain Christianity using the literary forms of the Greco-Roman world. A single excerpt in a letter attributed to Clement is the only evidence for the supposed and rather suspicious *Secret Gospel of Mark.* See also Smith, Morton.

Clement of Rome Overseer [bishop] of the Roman church; d. c. 99;

apostolic father and probable author of *1 Clement*. Roman Catholics view Clement as the fourth pope. See also apostolic fathers; *Clement, First*.

codex Plural *codices;* an ancient form of book. Pages were collected, stacked, and bound together, and both sides of the writing surface could be used, so the codex was more economical than the scroll for preserving texts. See also papyrus; scroll.

Codex Leicester Renaissance manuscript; collection of Leonardo Da Vinci's writings, also known as *Codex Hammer*. Dan Brown describes it as written on "parchment" (*DVC,* 300); in fact, Leonardo penned *Leicester* on linen paper. See also Leonardo da Vinci; Renaissance.

Codex Sinaiticus Fourth-century Greek manuscript of the Bible. So named because it was discovered on Mt. Sinai in the mid–1850s, *Sinaiticus* is probably one of fifty copies of the Scriptures commissioned by Emperor Constantine (done between 330 and 350). *Sinaiticus* contains the Septuagint version (Greek copy of originally Hebrew texts) of the Old Testament, the apocryphal books, the New Testament, and two non-canonical books from the New Testament era: *Epistle of Barnabas* and *Shepherd of Hermas*. See also apocrypha; *Barnabas, Epistle of;* Bible; canon; *Codex Vaticanus;* Constantine the Great; Greek; Hebrew; *Shepherd of Hermas*.

Codex Vaticanus Fourth-century Greek manuscript of the Bible. Copied between 300 and 340, so named because it's part of the Vatican Library, probably coming from Alexandria (Egypt). *Vaticanus* includes the Septuagint (Greek) version of the Old Testament as well as the apocryphal books; because several pages at the end are missing, no one knows whether *Epistle of Barnabas* or *Shepherd of Hermas* ever appeared in it. See also apocrypha; Bible; canon; *Codex Sinaiticus;* Greek.

Communion English translation of Greek *koinonia,* "fellowship." *Communion* (*DVC,* 236) most often refers to the Christian commemoration of the Last Supper, also known as "the Lord's Supper" or, in some traditions, "Eucharist" or "Mass." See *Last Supper*.

"companion," Aramaic word for *Da Vinci Code* reference to a word in the third-century Gnostic *Gospel of Philip,* referring to Mary Magdalene as the "companion" of Jesus. One of Dan Brown's characters says, "As any Aramaic scholar will tell you, the word *companion,* in those days, literally meant 'spouse'" (*DVC,* 246). However, the sole ancient manuscript of *Gospel of Philip* is written in Coptic, not Aramaic (found in 1945 at Nag Hammadi), and no evidence has been found to suggest that an Aramaic version ever existed. The word translated "companion" derives from the Greek *koinonos,* a term that never required sexual or marital relationship; in fact, it appears ten times in the Greek New Testament with no hint of a sexual relationship (Matt. 23:30; Luke 5:10; 1 Cor. 10:18, 20; 2 Cor. 1:7; 8:23; Philem. 1:17; Heb. 10:33; 1 Peter 5:1; 2 Peter 1:4). In addition, *Gospel of Philip's* language suggests the *opposite* of Brown's theory, thus providing no support to the notion that Jesus and Mary were married. See also Aramaic; Communion; Coptic; Greek; *Gospel of Philip;* Mary Magdalene; Nag Hammadi.

compass rose A navigational device that appeared in the fourteenth century; aligned with the globe's north-south (longitudinal) meridian, the rose indicates the eight—or sixteen or thirty-two—wind directions (*DVC,* 106). By Columbus's time, the rose was represented as the *fleur-de-lis,* and its frequent embellishment on manuscripts lends itself to esoteric 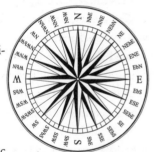 speculations—such as that at one time the prime meridian went through the Church of Saint-Sulpice in Paris. See also *fleur-de-lis;* prime meridian; Saint-Sulpice.

conspiracy The word's roots indicate "a breathing together" or "a harmony between" people. As generally used, it means an evil plot by a tightly connected group. Dan Brown alleges that the Catholic Church has engaged in a conspiracy (*DVC,* 169) to hide the truth about Jesus and Mary Magdalene, which his novel purposes to disclose.

Constantine the Great Roman Emperor (r. 306–337); claimed he became a Christian in 310, before the Battle at Milvian Bridge in Rome. In 313, he issued the Edict of Milan, recognizing Christianity as a legal (equally privileged) religion in the empire. *The Da Vinci Code* (see 125, 232) makes several claims about Constantine germane to Christian history:

- Dan Brown's Robert Langdon claims that "Constantine and his male successors successfully converted the world from matriarchal paganism to patriarchal Christianity" (*DVC*, 124). Actually, Constantine gave Christianity equal legal status with pagan religions; paganism persisted in the empire long after his reign. In fact, in the mid-fourth century, Julian, a pagan emperor, restored many pagan temples. Also, Roman paganism was *not* matriarchal—the chief deity was the male Jupiter (Zeus).
- Another character says that "the Bible, as we know it today, was collated by the pagan emperor Constantine the Great" (*DVC*, 231). In truth, Constantine had *nothing* to do with the selection or collation of the New Testament's twenty-seven books; by the late first and second centuries, Christians throughout the world had accepted twenty, including the four gospels, as authoritative guidelines for life. Debates about the other seven *did* persist into the fourth century; however, the final canon emerged from a consensus of church leaders, not from imperial decree. After the Council of Nicaea (325), Constantine authorized the copying and distribution of fifty Bibles, but the editions copied *before* these fifty do not differ significantly from the editions copied *after*.
- *The Da Vinci Code* also alleges that Constantine "was a lifelong pagan who was baptized on his deathbed, too weak to protest" (232). In this, Brown may be partially correct. Throughout his life, Constantine appears to have identified

CONSTANTINE

c. 280—born

306—became co-emperor

310—claimed conversion to Christianity

312—defeated Maxentius at Milvian Bridge

313—issued Edict of Milan

314—intervened in the Donatist controversy

323—finally defeated (and executed) co-emperor Licinius

Jesus Christ with the pagan deity *Sol Invictus* ("Invincible Sun"). Nevertheless, his baptism did not occur against his will; fourth-century baptisms were frequently slated for the time of physical death. (Constantine chose to be baptized by a bishop named Eusebius of Nicomedia.)

- Brown's Leigh Teabing charges that Constantine changed the day of Christian worship from Saturday to Sunday "to coincide with the pagan's veneration day of the sun" (*DVC,* 233). While Constantine did officially recognize Sunday as a day of rest, Christians had gathered on Sunday since the first century (see Acts 20:7). See also Athanasius of Alexandria; Bible; canon; *Codex Sinaiticus;* Council of Nicaea; Edict of Milan; goddess worship; paganism; Sabbath; *Sol Invictus.*

CONSTANTINE
(cont.)

324—chose Byzantium (renamed Constantinopolis) as empire's new capital; outlawed pagan sacrifice, banned gladiatorial contests, passed legislation against immorality, strengthened legislation against divorce

325—convened the Council of Nicaea, which condemned Arianism

326—executed his son Crispus

337—baptized by Eusebius, died of illness, interred at Church of the Holy Apostles

Coptic Ancient language descended from the earlier dialects of Egypt; flourished from the third century through the twelfth centuries. The Coptic alphabet is drawn primarily from Greek and looks much like it; many Greek loanwords appear in Coptic documents. In the third and fourth centuries, Coptic thrived in Egyptian religious communities, which included both Christian monasteries and Gnostic splinter groups. Coptic was the language of the Gnostic codices unearthed in 1945 near Nag Hammadi. See also codex; "companion," Aramaic word for; Greek; Nag Hammadi.

Coptic Apocalypse of Paul, The Late-second- to late-fourth-century Gnostic writing. Admittedly confusing is that this document differs radically from the fourth-century Christian writing known as *The Apocalypse of Paul. The Coptic Apocalypse of Paul* was found in fragmentary form at Nag Hammadi and describes Paul's supposed ascension through several levels of heaven. Like many Gnostic works, *The Coptic Apocalypse of Paul* presents a negative view of the Old Testament deity and was clearly not written by Paul. No early Christian writer considered this document to have any authority for believers or any place among the canonical Scriptures. See also *Apocalypse of Paul;* canon; Gnosticism; Nag Hammadi.

Coptic Apocalypse of Peter, The Late-third-century Gnostic writing, falsely ascribed to a prominent apostle; discovered at Nag Hammadi; frequently confused with the *The Apocalypse of Peter,* an early-second-century Christian text. *The Coptic Apocalypse of Peter* is a docetic writing, claiming that Jesus had no physical body: "The one whose hands and feet they nailed to the cross [was] only a fleshly substitute." No early Christian writer considered this document to have any authority for believers or any place among the canonical Scriptures. See also *Apocalypse of Peter;* canon; Docetism; Gnosticism; Nag Hammadi.

Coptic Gospel of the Egyptians, The Third- or fourth-century Gnostic writing; frequently confused with the earlier *Gospel of the Egyptians;* recounts a Gnostic myth in which Jesus is presented as a reincarnation of Seth, the third son of Adam and Eve. No early Christian writer considered this document to have any authority for believers or any place among the canonical Scriptures. See also Gnosticism; *Gospel of the Egyptians;* Nag Hammadi.

Coptic Museum In Cairo; current home of the Nag Hammadi library.

Corbu, Noël Entrepreneurial Frenchman who purchased the Rennes-le-Château estate in 1946; was perhaps inadvertently responsible for the Priory of Sion farce. In 1953, Corbu converted the property into a hotel and restaurant and began to tell a story of Bérenger Saunière, the priest of Rennes-le-Château who supposedly discovered a mysterious treasure during renovations of the village church in 1891. Corbu's story was eventually picked up by a newspaper; a transcript of his recorded interview still exists.

There is no historical account of this story before the 1950s, when Corbu began to tell it to his guests; there is, however, evidence that Corbu was acquainted with Pierre Plantard, and it may have been this relationship that provided Plantard with a story that would enhance his scheme. For him, the mysterious "discovery" by Saunière became documents that revealed the existence of a secret society protecting an even greater secret. Plantard told his story to the writers of *Holy Blood, Holy Grail,* but later admitted in court that he'd created the documents and the entire story. The fabricated Priory account found international visibility in *The Da Vinci Code.* See Plantard, Pierre; Priory of Sion; Rennes-le-Château; Saunière, Bérenger.

Corinthians, Third Also known as *3 Corinthians;* mid-second-century Christian writing that claims to be authentic correspondence between Paul and the Corinthians. This letter was part of a larger work entitled *The Acts of Paul.* See *Acts of Paul.*

Council of Carthage Regional gathering of North African church leaders in 397; also known as the Third Council of Carthage, to distinguish it from two previous gatherings in the same city. At Carthage, several leaders identified as "divine Scripture" the same books that appear in New Testaments today. See also Athanasius of Alexandria; Bible; canon.

Council of Hippo Regional gathering of North African church leaders in 393; the group recognized the twenty-seven New Testament writings as the authoritative guidelines for their churches' faith and practice. See also Athanasius of Alexandria; Bible; canon.

Council of Nicaea Gathering of church leaders in Nicaea, a town at the site of modern Iznik (northwest Turkey), in 325. According to Dan Brown, "Until [the Council of Nicaea], Jesus was viewed by his followers as a mortal prophet . . . a great and powerful man, but a *man* nonetheless. A mortal" (233). *The Da Vinci Code's* Leigh Teabing claims that "Jesus' establishment as 'the Son of God' was officially proposed and voted on by the Council of Nicaea . . . [and] a relatively close vote at that" (233); this vote, allegedly, turned Jesus into an "unchallengeable" deity and made salvation available only through "the Roman Catholic Church" (233). Constantine supposedly convened the Council because Christians and pagans were fighting, and he wanted "to unify Rome under a single religion, Christianity" (*DVC,* 232). These claims are riddled with historical errors.

- First, Constantine called the Council because two different groups of *Christians,* the Arians and the orthodox, were disputing.
- Second, the Council's purpose was neither to unify the empire under a

single religion nor to declare Jesus divine; it was, rather, to seek a consensus among Christians regarding what the Scriptures teach about Jesus Christ. A North African elder named Arius had claimed that Jesus was a created being, not God in human flesh; the bishops in Nicaea summarized their shared commitment that from the beginning believers had rightly held that Jesus was uniquely God. According to a letter written by an eyewitness: "Although some declared and confessed that they believed things that were contrary to the divinely-inspired Scriptures . . . more than three hundred bishops unanimously confirmed one and the same faith, which according to the truth and the legitimate interpretation of God's law is *the* faith."

- Third, the Roman Catholic Church as we know it today—with a hierarchy of bishops, archbishops, and a bishop of bishops (the pope)—emerged gradually over hundreds of years, not all at once (at Nicaea or anywhere else). The truly *Roman* Catholic Church did not exist in its present form until well after this Council.

- Finally, the Council's vote *wasn't* close: Out of over three hundred church leaders, only two refused to sign the Nicene Creed, which described Jesus as "true God from true God." See also Arius of Alexandria; Athanasius of Alexandria; Christology; Constantine the Great; Jesus as Son of God; Roman Catholic Church.

cross Ancient Roman instrument used for the torture and execution of criminals. The New Testament accounts say that Jesus was crucified on a *stauros* (Greek: "cross" or "execution-stake"), the exact shape of which is uncertain—it may have been a single piece of wood driven into the ground, or it may have been two pieces of wood bound or fastened together to form either an X, a T, or the dagger-like cross familiar to most Christians. One of Dan Brown's characters muses that he "was always surprised how few Christians who gazed upon the 'crucifix' realized their symbol's violent history was reflected in its very name: 'cross' and 'crucifix' came from the Latin verb *cruciare*—to torture" (*DVC*, 145).

In this, *The Da Vinci Code* is technically correct—that is where the word *cross* originates (its other root is the Latin *crux,* "device for torture"). The symbol of the cross was not, however, intended to encourage Chris-

tians to torture those who held conflicting beliefs; its aim was to encourage remembrance of the sufferings Jesus endured "once for all" for
humanity's sins (Rom. 6:10; Heb. 7:27; 9:12; 10:10; cf. 1 Peter 3:18).
Interestingly, the earliest symbol used to signify Christian faith wasn't a
cross but a fish—crosses didn't emerge as such until the mid-fifth century,
when believers inscribed equal-armed crosses on Christian tombs in
Rome. The T-shaped and dagger-shaped crosses began to be used as
Christian symbols in the seventh century. See also crucifix; cruciform;
equal-armed cross; Latin cross.

Crowley, Aleister Born in England to religious parents; d. 1947; grew up
to be skeptical of Christianity and eventually created Thelema, a philosophy that incorporated teachings and rituals from ancient and modern religions. Thelema teaches that an individual's own will is the law that
governs their life; love is most often equated with sex, and sexual union is
one way participants (two or more) can experience true spirituality—a
belief that parallels *The Da Vinci Code*'s presentation of *Hieros Gamos*
(309).

Crowley's image appears on the cover of the Beatles' *Sgt. Pepper's
Lonely Hearts Club Band*, on Led Zeppelin's fourth album, and on
Michael Jackson's *Dangerous*. His writings (like *The Equinox* and *The
Diary of a Drug Fiend*), often recognized as clever and stylish, remain
iconic and influential among followers of the occult; his life still stirs controversy and discussion. Notorious for radical sexual ideas and irreverent
behavior, his own mother called him "the Beast" and, as an adult, he
accepted the title for himself. He died addicted to heroin and bankrupt.
See also *Hieros Gamos*.

crucifix From Latin *cruciare*, "to torture" (*DVC*, 37, 145). Symbol or structure bearing an image of Jesus crucified. The crucifix began to be widely
seen in Roman Catholic churches in the thirteenth century. See also cross;
cruciform; equal-armed cross.

cruciform Anything cross-shaped is "cruciform," and many churches are
designed to represent this sacred symbol (*DVC*, 33). In *The Da Vinci
Code*, French Police Chief Bezu Fache's tie clip is cruciform; Robert Langdon and Sophie Neveu also obtain entry to a Swiss bank safety deposit

box with a cruciform key. See also cross; crucifix.

Crusades, The Series of military campaigns; 1095–1291; *crusade* literally means "religious war." Dan Brown says one goal of the Crusades was to destroy evidence that Jesus and Mary Magdalene had been married (*DVC*, 254). There is no reliable historical evidence for this claim.

In the eleventh century, rumors began to circulate in Europe that Muslim marauders were harassing Christian pilgrims on their way to Jerusalem. Muslim warlords *did* charge high tariffs when pilgrims crossed into their territories; even so, harassment was not widespread. Nevertheless, when Emperor Alexius I of the Eastern (Byzantine) Roman Empire asked Pope Urban II to assist him in his struggle, the pope responded eagerly. At a council in the French city of Clermont, Urban II urged nobles, knights, and knaves to undertake a crusade against the Muslims, declaring at the climax of his speech, "All who die, by the way, whether by land or by sea, or in battle against the pagans, shall have immediate remission of sins. This I grant them through the power of God!" To this, the crowd responded, *"Deus volt!"* ("God wills it!"). A total of nine crusades were ultimately directed against the Muslims.

- *First Crusade (1095–1099):* Crusader armies went east and conquered Jerusalem, expelling Muslims from the Holy Land while slaughtering thousands of Muslims, Jews, and Eastern Orthodox Christians in the city.
- *Second Crusade (1147–1149):* Urged by Bernard of Clairvaux, French and German armies marched across Asia Minor and attacked Damascus. Failing to conquer, both armies returned to Europe.
- *Third Crusade (1187–1191):* In 1187, Muslim leader Saladin recaptured Jerusalem; Richard the Lionhearted of England, Philip II of France, and Holy Roman Emperor Frederick I led the Third Crusade to recapture it. Frederick drowned en route, and Philip returned to France after the crusaders captured the seaport Acre. The remaining crusaders were unable to reach Jerusalem; Richard negotiated peace with Saladin and returned to England.
- *Fourth Crusade (1202–1204):* Initiated by Pope Innocent III, who intended to invade the Holy Land through Egypt. The onslaught was diverted northward into Asia Minor where—on Good Friday, 1204—frustrated crusaders pillaged Constantinople, murdering, robbing, and

raping thousands of Eastern Orthodox Christians.

- *Fifth Crusade (1215–1219):* Crusaders from Hungary, Austria, and Bavaria attempted to capture Cairo. Nile flooding forced them to surrender.

- *Sixth Crusade (1228–1229):* Through diplomacy and without the pope's support, Holy Roman Emperor Frederick II established a ten-year truce between Christians and Muslims in Jerusalem. The truce expired in 1239, and Egyptian Muslims reconquered the city five years later.

- *Seventh Crusade (1249–1252):* Following the fall of Jerusalem, King Louis IX of France launched a failed crusade against Egypt, after which the French withdrew.

- *Eighth Crusade (1270):* Louis IX's second campaign against the Egyptians was diverted to Tunisia, where he died.

- *Ninth Crusade (1271):* The future King Edward I of England led this failed crusade against Muslims in Syria.

In 1291, the last crusader stronghold—the seaport Acre—fell to a Muslim army. The last order of crusading knights, the Knights Hospitaller, fled to the island of Rhodes and then to Malta. The Knights remained on Malta until they were defeated by France's Napoleon Bonaparte in 1798.

Despite the nobility and chivalry associated with the crusaders in the imaginations of many, their cruelty poisoned relationships between Western Christians and Eastern Orthodox Christians, Muslims, and Jews for centuries. On March 12, 2000, Pope John Paul II, on behalf of the Roman Catholic Church, asked forgiveness for wrongs committed during the Crusades. See also Godefroi de Bouillon; Holy Roman Empire; Knights Hospitaller.

crux gemmata Frequently fork-ended "gemmed cross" with thirteen gems (to represent Christ and the twelve disciples), usually ornate and valuable. Often viewed as an ideogram for its symbolic aspects (*DVC,* 25).

cryptex Device first found in *The Da Vinci Code;* fictitiously invented by Leonardo da Vinci (there is no evidence he ever conceived such an object) and resurrected by Sophie's grandfather to hide secret documents

(*DVC,* 198–200). Web sites now sell artistic, creative reproductions of the cryptex.

cryptography The discipline of studying encrypted texts. Encryption is the process through which a readable text is transformed into a code that conceals its meaning. A cryptographer (like *Da Vinci Code*'s Sophie Neveu) must discern the "key," or encryption method, that will reveal how to read the text (*DVC,* 49). The word *cryptex* (199), derived from *cryptography,* was introduced in this novel.

Cullmann, Oscar Renowned New Testament scholar; d. 1999; professor of New Testament and Early Church History at the Sorbonne, Basel Reformed Seminary, and University of Strasbourg; known for his tireless efforts to achieve peace between Lutherans and Roman Catholics. In an article entitled "Infancy Gospels," Cullmann contended that the longer a gospel was written after the time of Jesus, the less likely it was to recount the historical truth about him (*New Testament Apocrypha,* ed. Wilhelm Schneemelcher): "The further we move in time from the beginnings, the more unrestrained becomes the application to Jesus of what is recounted about the birth and infancy of sons of gods and children of supernatural origin." As such, the earliest gospels—Matthew, Mark, Luke, and John—are the writings that are most likely to reflect historically accurate understanding. See also Gospels, canonical.

da Vinci, Leonardo See Leonardo da Vinci.

Da Vinci Code, The Mirroring much of its content, the novel's title itself contains a historical error. Leonardo da Vinci is not referred to by scholars and others as "Da Vinci" but as "Leonardo," in the same way that Michelangelo Buonarroti is known as "Michelangelo" and Sandro Botticelli is known as "Botticelli." "Da Vinci" as part of his name refers to the town of his father, meaning "from the town of Vinci."

Furthermore, because—much to the disappointment of conspiracy theorists—there is no credible evidence that Leonardo had a "code," *The Da Vinci Code* would be more appropriately titled *The Dan Brown Code*.

Da Vinci Code Deception, The: Fact vs. Fiction—Your Guide to the Truth. DVD; Grizzly Adams Productions, Inc; David W. Balsiger, Producer.

Da Vinci Code literature/media The advent of Dan Brown's *The Da Vinci Code* has wrought an outpouring of writings, many of which challenge his revisions of history, theology, and art. Examples include:

- Abanes, Richard, *The Truth Behind the Da Vinci Code*
- Balsiger, David W., producer (DVD), *Breaking The Da Vinci Code: Answers to the Questions Everyone Is Asking*
- Balsiger, David W., producer (DVD), *The Da Vinci Code Deception: Fact vs. Fiction—Your Guide to the Truth.*
- Berstein, Peter W., and Annalyn Swan, eds., *Secrets of the Da Vinci Code: The Unauthorized Guide to the Bestselling Novel* (*U.S. News and World Report,* Collector's Edition [2/22/05])
- Bock, Darrell L., *Breaking the Da Vinci Code*

- Cox, Simon, *Cracking the Da Vinci Code: The Unauthorized Guide to the Facts Behind Dan Brown's Bestselling Novel* (essentially pro-*DVC*; different from Garlow and Jones's *Cracking Da Vinci's Code*; advocate of "alternative" history)
- Ehrman, Bart D., *Truth and Fiction in The Da Vinci Code: A Historian Reveals What We Can Really Know About Jesus, Mary, and Constantine*
- *Exposing the Da Vinci Code* (DVD; produced by Highland Entertainment [essentially opposes *The Da Vinci Code*; see *Unlocking Da Vinci's Code: Mystery or Conspiracy?*])
- Garlow, James L., and Peter Jones, *Cracking Da Vinci's Code* (not to be confused with Cox's *Cracking the Da Vinci Code*)
- Haag, Michael and Veronica, *The Rough Guide to The Da Vinci Code*
- Hanegraaff, Hank, and Paul Maier, *The Da Vinci Code: Fact or Fiction?*
- Jones, Timothy Paul, *Answers to The Da Vinci Code*
- Kellmeyer, Steven, *Fact and Fiction in The Da Vinci Code*
- Lutzer, Erwin W., *The Da Vinci Code Deception: Credible Answers to the Questions Millions Are Asking About Jesus, the Bible, and The Da Vinci Code*
- Miesel, Sandra, and Carl E. Olson, *The Da Vinci Code Hoax*
- Newman, Sharan, *The Real History Behind The Da Vinci Code*
- *Secrets to the Code* (NBC News, *Dateline NBC* [4/13/05: Transcript 1762])
- *Unlocking Da Vinci's Code: Mystery or Conspiracy?* (DVD; produced by Highland Entertainment [essentially supports *The Da Vinci Code*; see *Exposing the Da Vinci Code*])
- Wellborn, Amy, *De-Coding Da Vinci: The Facts Behind the Fiction of The Da Vinci Code*
- Witherington III, Ben, *The Gospel Code: Novel Claims About Jesus, Mary Magdalene, and Da Vinci*

Dagobert II One of Merovingian King Dagobert's descendants was Godefroi de Bouillon, supposed founder of the Priory of Sion (*DVC*, 258). Dan Brown has one character say that when Dagobert II was murdered, his son Sigisbert IV escaped execution, so his royal line survived. This is incorrect. Dagobert II died in 679, Childeric III was the only surviving Merovingian, and he was overthrown in 751. In addition, Brown wrongly claims the Merovingians founded Paris, which was a small village the

Romans expanded into a city long before the Merovingians ruled it. See also Godefroi de Bouillon; Merovingian; Paris; Priory of Sion.

Daniel Old Testament book; the Greek version, found in the Roman Catholic and Eastern Orthodox Bibles, is longer than the Hebrew version, found in Jewish and Protestant Bibles. See also Bible; canon.

David, House of The descendents of King David, including Jesus, were considered of the "House of David," a frequent scriptural term. Dan Brown correctly uses it to refer to the genealogy of Jesus, but mistakenly refers to "the House of Benjamin" as being powerful (*DVC*, 248–49), which he believed made the alleged marriage of Jesus to Mary Magdalene a fusion of "two royal bloodlines" and the creation of "a potent political union."

Four problems: (1) There is no credible evidence that Jesus was married; (2) the small House of Benjamin was not powerful; (3) Benjamin was not "royal"; (4) there is no evidence that Mary Magdalene was a Benjaminite. See Benjamin, tribe of; Mary Magdalene.

Dead Sea Scrolls, The Ancient writings, copied between the second century BC and AD 68; collection of more than eight hundred documents, including texts from the Hebrew Bible, discovered from 1947 to 1956 near the ruins of the ancient village of Qumran, near the Dead Sea. Dan Brown says that the Dead Sea Scrolls, which he mistakenly groups with the writings from Nag Hammadi,

- tell "the true Grail story";
- "speak of Christ's ministry in very human terms";
- represent "the earliest Christian records"; and
- "do not match up with the Gospels in the Bible" (*DVC*, 245–46).

Actually:

- The Scrolls never mention the Holy Grail, a legend that didn't emerge for another millennium (late 1100s), in a novel by Chretien de Troyes.
- They don't describe Jesus "in very human terms."
- They aren't Christian records at all—they're *Jewish* writings, most of which originated centuries before Christ's birth. The Scrolls seem to

have been copied by a small Jewish sect known as the Essenes, who probably hid them during the conflict with the Romans that culminated in the burning of the Jewish temple in AD 70. Approximately one-third of the texts are copies of Old Testament Scriptures; another third are traditional Jewish stories (including various accounts of Enoch's life) and commentaries on Old Testament books; the rest relate to the daily life of the Essene community.

Jose O'Callaghan and Carsten Peter Thiede contend that a fragment known as 7Q5 comes from Mark's gospel. Few scholars have accepted their arguments, but even if they're correct, the fragment would prove anything but scandalous, as it would come from a New Testament gospel. See also *Enoch, Book of;* Essenes; Holy Grail; Nag Hammadi; Qumran; temple, Herod's.

December 25 Date of the winter solstice celebration among ancient Romans; the supposed birthday of *Sol Invictus,* Osiris, Jupiter, and Mithras (*DVC,* 232). Christians converted from paganism probably began to celebrate the birth of Jesus on December 25, in the late fourth century; according to the contemporary church father John Chrysostom, the custom reached Antioch of Syria around 375. See Christianity as "borrowed"; church fathers; *Sol Invictus.*

deconstructionism An approach to reading a text that tries to discern all hidden opinions, influences, agendas, and philosophies motivating its author; part of a larger academic approach called "literary criticism." Opponents of deconstructionism claim that this method suggests all information to be relative and is merely a way to strip from a text all authority and meaning. In other words, deconstructionism holds that the author's intended meaning can't simply be what it is—what the author meant becomes whatever the text means to each individual reader. *The Da Vinci Code's* Leigh Teabing arrives at the conclusion that "history" is relative because those in power (the "winners") are its writers, so historical accounts, intrinsically, cannot be trusted as accurate (*DVC,* 256).

Depository Bank of Zurich The bank in Dan Brown's novel (*DVC,* 171) is a fictitious institution, housing a safety deposit box that can be opened with a "cruciform key" shaped like a pre-Christian cross and allegedly representing peace (for Switzerland as a neutral nation). Nevertheless, the bona fide Depository Bank of Zurich, established in 1967, is a *Geldschrank Banke* that specializes in the secret accounts often associated with Swiss banking.

deuterocanonical Term (from Greek) that means "from the second canon." See apocrypha.

"Deutero-Pauline" Epistles, The New Testament-studies term referring to the biblical books of Ephesians, Colossians, 2 Thessalonians; used by scholars who deny that the apostle Paul wrote these letters, which straightforwardly claim to be from Paul. Although the writing style does differ from Paul's other writings, the best evidence suggests that he penned them, perhaps through a scribe. For presentations of this evidence, see A. Van Roon's *The Authenticity of Ephesians,* N. T. Wright's *Colossians and Philemon,* and Leon Morris's *The First and Second Epistles to the Thessalonians.* See also Pastoral Epistles; Pauline corpus.

Dialogue of the Savior Mid-second-century Gnostic writing; a list of supposed sayings of Jesus. Although some portions originated in the first century, the book's contents as found at Nag Hammadi clearly reflect second-century Gnostic teachings and demonstrate an extremely negative view of women. When one of the disciples asked, "When we pray, how should we pray?" Jesus is said to have replied, "Pray in a place where there are no women." Another disciple then allegedly understands this statement as a call to "destroy the works of womanhood." No early Christian writer considered *Dialogue of the Savior* to have any authority for believers or any place among the canonical Scriptures. See also Gnosticism; Nag Hammadi.

Diatessaron Greek term meaning "by means of four"; a one-volume harmony of the four canonical gospels, prepared between 160 and 175 by Tatian, a Syrian believer trained in the Christian faith by Justin Martyr. Syrian churches copied and used *Diatessaron* for centuries after its completion.

Dan Brown implies that "more than eighty" gospels were considered for New Testament inclusion and that the four canonical gospels were selected in the fourth century (*DVC,* 231–34). However, that Tatian used only the four canonical gospels when he compiled *Diatessaron* more than one hundred fifty years earlier demonstrates that Christians recognized Matthew, Mark, Luke, and John as authoritative at least a hundred years before Constantine was even born. See also canon; Constantine the Great; Gospels, canonical; Justin Martyr.

Didache Greek, "teaching"; *Didache* is a shortened form of the full title, *The Teaching of the Lord to the Gentiles Through the Twelve Apostles* (also known as *The Judgment of Peter*); an early Christian manual of church order probably written in the late first century. According to Eusebius, some early Christians accepted *Didache* as part of the New Testament canon, and although completely orthodox and in agreement with the canonical New Testament, it was eventually excluded, possibly because it could not be clearly connected to an apostle.

Didache's first section—entitled "Two Ways"—describes the lifestyle choices that should distinguish Christians from nonbelievers; this section is duplicated (with minor variations) in *Epistle of Barnabas.* The second section describes proper procedures for administering baptism and the Lord's Supper, and the final section outlines the habits expected of church leaders, especially traveling prophets and evangelists.

Three times *Didache* refers to Jesus as "Son of God" (9:3, 6; 10:2), disproving Dan Brown's claim that "Jesus' establishment as the 'Son of God' was officially proposed and voted on" at Nicaea in 325 (233). See Council of Nicaea; *Epistle of Barnabas;* Eusebius of Caesarea; Jesus as Son of God.

disciple English translation of the Greek *mathetes,* "learner" or "follower"; in first-century Jewish usage, one whose life is committed to imitating a certain rabbi; in Christian usage, one whose life is entrusted to following Jesus Christ. Jesus defined a disciple's calling in this way: "If anyone would come after me, he must deny himself and take up his cross and follow me. For whoever wants to save his life will lose it, but whoever loses his life for me and for the gospel will save it" (Mark 8:34–35).

Discipline, The Knotted whip designed for self-mortification (*DVC,* 14). Josemaria Escrivá, founder of Opus Dei, suggested that followers control their passions and material desires by flagellating their own flesh; the Discipline is a device approved for this purpose. See also *Castigo corpus meum.*

Divine Proportion, The (PHI) Mathematical term; irrational number, beginning 1.61803 . . . ; typically symbolized by the Greek letter *phi;* also known as the Golden Ratio, Golden Mean, Golden Section, and *Sectio Divina.* Two lengths—designated *a* and *b*—are said to be in Divine Proportion when *a* + *b* is to *a* as *a* is to *b;* the ratio describing the relationship of the two lengths to each other is 1:1.61803. . . .

A Dan Brown character asserts that the Divine Proportion, found throughout art and nature, explains the proportions of male and female bees in a hive, of the human body, of great paintings and buildings, etc. (*DVC,* 93–97). While the Divine Pro-

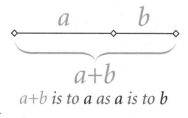

$a+b$ is to a as a is to b

portion is frequently found in art and nature, several errors mar *The Da Vinci Code*'s presentation. For example: Brown presents the proportion as the rational number 1.618 instead of the irrational 1.61803 . . . ; the proportion of male to female bees in a hive is closer to 1:1.9; a person with a navel in accord with Divine Proportion would be very oddly proportioned (on most, the ratio that represents the navel's placement relative to the rest of the body is 1:1.7). See also Fibonacci Sequence; *Sectio Divina.*

Docetism From Greek *dokein,* "to seem"; the belief that Jesus only seemed human. Because the Gnostics viewed the physical world as evil, they could not accept that Jesus was both fully divine and fully human; as such, most Gnostics were also docetists. Dan Brown's *Da Vinci Code* appeal to Gnostic sources for Jesus being a human prophet married to Mary Magdalene clearly contradicts historical facts. See also Cathari; Christology; Gnosticism.

Dossiers Secrets, Les Lists of genealogies forged by Pierre Plantard, as well as other documents planted in the National Library of France in order to prove Plantard's association with French royal bloodlines (*DVC,* 206, 326). Later found bogus. See also Bibliothèque Nationale de France; Plantard, Pierre.

Draconian Devil, O Anagram for "Leonardo da Vinci." Early in *The Da Vinci Code,* Louvre curator Jacques Saunière's body is found along with a mysterious message, one line of which is "O, Draconian Devil" (*DVC,* 43–44).

Ebionites From Hebrew *ebionim,* "poor ones"; a Jewish sect that recognized Jesus as Messiah, but believed that God adopted him as his Son at his baptism. The only Scripture they used seems to have been an altered version of the gospel of Matthew known as *Gospel of the Ebionites.* They revered the blood relatives of Jesus and regarded James, his brother, as their patron apostle. See also Adoptionism; Christology; *Gospel of the Ebionites; Gospel of the Hebrews; Gospel of the Nazoreans.*

Ecclesiasticus Alternate name for the apocryphal *Wisdom of Sirach.* See apocrypha; *Wisdom of Sirach.*

Edict of Milan, The Roman imperial decree, issued by Constantine of the Western empire and Licinius of the Eastern empire in 313, that gave Christianity and paganism equal status. Although the edict technically ended Roman persecution of Christians, it did not make Christianity the empire's official religion. Christianity gained that status near the end of the fourth century. See also Constantine the Great; Theodosius I.

Egerton Papyrus, The Fragments from a first- or second-century document sometimes known as *The Egerton Gospel* (also known as "Papyrus Egerton II"); it's not known whether these were originally part of a complete gospel. The papyrus includes four stories about Jesus, three of which, in different forms, appear in the canonical Gospels (Mark 1:40–45; 12:13–17; John 5:39–47; 10:33–39), and one of which—where Jesus stretches out his hand toward the Jordan River and talks about the bearing of fruit—does not have a gospel parallel. No quotations from the Egerton Papyrus appear in any early Christian writings; as such, there is simply not enough information available to make definite judgments about it. See also Bible; canon; Gospels, canonical.

Ehrman, Bart D. Author and scholar who has responded to many issues raised by Dan Brown in a book entitled *Truth and Fiction in The Da Vinci Code: A Historian Reveals What We Can Really Know about Jesus, Mary, and Constantine.* Also author of *Misquoting Jesus: The Story Behind Who Changed the Bible and Why; Jesus: Apocalyptic Prophet of the New Millennium; The New Testament: A Historical Introduction to the Early Christian Writings; The New Testament and Other Early Christian Writings: A Reader; The Orthodox Corruption of Scripture: The Effect of Early Christological Controversies on the Text of the New Testament; After the New Testament: A Reader in Early Christianity.* Ehrman does seek to rehabilitate "Christian Gnosticism" as a valid expression of early Christianity.

Eisler, Riane Author of *The Chalice and the Blade: Our History, Our Future;* President of the Center for Partnership Studies. Eisler is a proponent of the feminist interpretation of Mary Magdalene.

El Hebrew title meaning "God" or "Mighty One." Used in the Jewish Scriptures to refer to the one true God; also used for deities of other nations.

Elohim Hebrew title for God; primarily used in the Hebrew Scriptures to refer to the one true God. That *Elohim* is technically the plural form of *El* does not imply there is more than one God; the term describes a *plurality of majesty* and, specifically, a *plurality of oneness,* as seen from God's words in Genesis 1:26–27. See also *Adonai; YHWH.*

Enoch, The Book of Jewish writing (also known as *1 Enoch*); a five-part expansion on the brief biblical reference to the mysterious "Nephilim" (Gen. 6:1–4). *The Book of Enoch* was familiar to several church fathers, including Justin Martyr, Irenaeus, and Clement of Alexandria, and it appears in the Old Testament canon of the Ethiopian Orthodox (Tewahedo) Church. Despite the book's purported connection to Enoch (Gen. 5:18–24), its style and grammar point to a composition date around 160 BC.

Jude quoted *The Book of Enoch* (1 Enoch 1:9): "See, the Lord is coming with thousands upon thousands of his holy ones to judge everyone, and to convict all the ungodly of all the ungodly acts they have done in the ungodly way, and of all the harsh words ungodly sinners have spoken against him" (Jude 14–15). This (or similar citations) does not necessarily indicate that Jude or the church fathers viewed *Book of Enoch* as part of the biblical canon; for instance, the apostle Paul quoted the pagan prophet Epimenides at least twice (Acts 17:28; Titus 1:12), yet he certainly didn't view Epimenides' prophecies as canonical. See also apocrypha; Bible; canon.

Epiphanius of Salamis Church father; d. 402; author of *Panarion* (Greek, "medicine cabinet"), a handbook listing eighty teachings he considered to be heresies. Some scholars believe certain descriptions may have relied on exaggerated stories about these heresies; others take the reports at face value because Epiphanius says that as a youth he actively participated in a Gnostic group. His testimony is invaluable for his personal experience and for his references to books that have since been lost. See *Gospel of Eve; Gospel of the Hebrews;* heresy.

epistle From the Greek *epistole,* "letter." Archaic term for a letter.

Epistle of Barnabas See *Barnabas, Epistle of.*

equal-armed cross *The Da Vinci Code*'s Robert Langdon describes the equal-armed cross emblem, found on the mysterious deposit-box key, as a "symbol of peace" (*DVC,* 145). Also called a "cross formy," this image was used on the tunics of other military monks, such as the pope's own order, known as the Knights of the Holy Sepulchre. The equal-armed (equilateral) cross's ancient meanings are lost, but its earliest known symbolic usage is as a representative for the sun, not of peace.

Langdon contrasts this emblem with the traditional Christian cross, depicted only as an instrument representing an ancient Roman method of torture and execution (*DVC,* 145). Accordingly, Dan Brown's presentation bypasses more complex theological symbolism: The *crucifix* is a cross bearing the image of Jesus Christ, memorializing his sacrificial death. For believers, this suffering, this loss of life, is a remembrance of the Savior's saving act. A plain (or empty) cross with a longer vertical line (or a T-shaped Latin cross) represents the resurrection: Christ's victory over suffering and death. See also cross; crucifix; Latin cross.

eschatology Subfield of theology, from Greek *eschatologos;* based on the words *eschatos* and *logos,* meaning "the study of last things," "the final word." The study of how God may bring the present world to an end.

Escrivá de Balaguer, Josemaria Spanish priest; d. 1975; his devotion led him in 1928 to establish Opus Dei, literally, devoted to the "work of God" (Latin). Opus Dei is primarily focused on education and evangelism; it is not (as Dan Brown indicates) a "religious order" but a layman's organization with only a few priests involved. Escriva himself, concerned mostly with the "apostolate of the mind," endeavored to promote ultra-conservative Catholic doctrine; in 1990, he was declared a saint by Pope John Paul II. *The Da Vinci Code* portrays Opus Dei itself in ominous and sinister terms; in the novel, its representatives are baited into facilitating the machinations of a pervasive Catholic conspiracy. Little that Brown says about Opus Dei is accurate (*DVC,* 28). See Opus Dei.

Esdras, First Ancient apocryphal writing, accepted by the Eastern Orthodox Church as part of the Old Testament. See apocrypha; Bible; canon.

Esdras, Second Ancient apocryphal writing, accepted by the Russian (Slavonic) Orthodox and Ethiopian Orthodox Churches as part of the Old Testament. For some, the canonical books of Ezra and Nehemiah are called *1* and *2 Esdras,* respectively; among these Christians, *1* and *2 Esdras* are known as *3* and *4 Esdras,* respectively. See apocrypha; Bible; canon.

Essenes This term perhaps comes from the Aramaic *Issi'im,* "pious ones"; an ascetic Jewish sect that flourished along the Dead Sea from the mid-second century BC until the First Jewish-Roman War (AD 66–73). According to the Jewish historian Josephus, the Essenes were one of four sociopolitical groups in first-century Judaism, along with the Pharisees, the Sadducees, and the Zealots.

The Essenes seem to have been devout Jews that retreated into isolation in response to widespread priestly corruption (the post of high priest, rather than being regarded hereditarily, had been "purchased" by the Hasmonean family). The Essenes lived simply, faithfully following the Torah as well as their own communal laws, awaiting the time when "pure worship" would be restored in the Jewish temple. Apparently, during the war, the Essenes fled from their desert communities and hid their documents in caves near Qumran; these began to be found in the 1940s and became known as the Dead Sea Scrolls.

According to Dan Brown, the Essene documents "speak of Christ's ministry in very human terms," "highlight glaring historical discrepancies and fabrications" in the canonical Scriptures, and confirm "that the Bible was compiled and edited by men who possessed a political agenda" (*DVC*, 234). The Qumran writings, however, were primarily *pre*-Christian (BC) Jewish documents; indirect references to Christ are in copies of Old Testament writings (such as Isaiah, who doesn't name Jesus Christ but rather prophetically tells of Messiah's coming). Furthermore, far from highlighting "glaring discrepancies," the Qumran literature proves that the Old Testament Scriptures had been preserved from ancient times with remarkable accuracy. See also Dead Sea Scrolls; Josephus, Flavius; Pharisees; Qumran; Sadducees.

Dead Sea Area

Esther Old Testament historical book; the Greek version (in Roman Catholic and Eastern Orthodox Bibles) is longer than the Hebrew version (in Jewish and Protestant Bibles). See also apocrypha; Bible; canon.

Eusebius of Caesarea Christian historian; d. 339; known as "the father of church history"; also known as Eusebius Pamphilii ("Eusebius, friend of Pamphilus"); authored important works such as *Historia Ecclesiastica* ("Church History") and *Vita Constantini* ("Life of Constantine"). As a friend of Constantine, Eusebius was frequently caught up in the political maneuverings that marred the fourth-century church, and his writings often seemed to reflect an overly positive view of the emperor and his supposed faith. Nevertheless, the works of Eusebius remain invaluable, primarily because they included careful and extensive quotations from many early Christian writings that have since been lost. See also church fathers; Constantine the Great.

Eve First female in creation (Gen. 1–3); "the mother of all living." Dan Brown's Robert Langdon explains that scriptural teachings depict women as untrustworthy from the beginning, since it was Eve who convinced Adam to eat from the tree of knowledge, and that the pain associated with childbirth was a just punishment to her female descendants (*DVC*, 124). This doesn't tell the whole story: God gave the commandment not to eat forbidden fruit to Adam, so the first disobedience belonged to the man, and the apostle Paul states that sin entered the world through one man, Adam (Rom. 5:12–17). In the Genesis creation narrative (1:1–2:25), which moves from lower and simpler forms of life to higher and more intricate beings, Eve represented the high point of God's creation; at no point does Genesis suggest (as *The Da Vinci Code* claims—125, 238, 425) that Eve alone was viewed as responsible for original sin or for "the downfall of the human race." *Both* Adam and Eve were held responsible for their actions.

Evola, Julius Cesare Andrea Italian aristocrat, soldier, mountaineer, and writer; immersed himself in occult practices as well as philosophy; d. 1974; wrote *Revolt Against the Modern World;* deeply influenced by Friedrich Nietzsche; influenced Pierre Plantard. Considered by some to be the "godfather" of Italian Fascism, Evola enjoyed the favor and protection of

Benito Mussolini, and he translated neo-pagan and Masonic texts for Nazi leader Heinrich Himmler, who was devising rituals for his elite SS. See Plantard, Pierre.

exegesis In contrast to *eisegesis* (reading "into" a text one's own preferences), *exegesis* is the discipline of investigating and interpreting the facts coming "out of" a text, most generally the Bible. Particularly at stake is the truth contained in a passage—rightly understanding it, as expressed in an ancient language, and then explaining it. The exegete must appreciate the importance of a writer's literal meaning while also sensing (and evoking in translation) any allegorical or poetical elements therein. All supportable and tenable meaning found in biblical passages must be true to the author's intent and then made coherent and relevant to latter-day hearers. Notable exegetes include ancient scholars such as Ambrose and Augustine as well as Reformation giants like Martin Luther and John Calvin.

Exposing The Da Vinci Code DVD; produced by Highland Entertainment.

Exum, J. Cheryl Professor of Biblical Studies at the University of Sheffield; author of *Fragmented Women: Feminist Subversions of Biblical Narratives.*

fathers, the See church fathers.

female icons Icons—specifically, one-dimensional portraits of Christ, the apostles, and the saints—have a rich history in the Christian church, especially in Eastern Orthodoxy, which regards them as pictorial "windows to heaven." In contemporary culture, the term "female icon" refers to heroines of recent decades—for example, film stars like Liz Taylor and political figures like Eleanor Roosevelt.

In *The Da Vinci Code*'s focus on the "sacred feminine," such icons as "windows to heaven" fit the author's endeavor to enshrine Mary Magdalene as a ranked member of the Christian pantheon. Dan Brown significantly alters the meaning of "female icon," transforming Christ's cup from the Last Supper—the chalice that in medieval legends became the "Holy Grail"—into a sacred-feminine symbol. In this vein, the chalice—referring to Mary Magdalene's womb and, by extension, to Mary Magdalene herself—serves as a "female icon."

female leadership in the early church Some feminist writers contend that fragmentary bits of third-century writings like *The Gospel of Thomas* indicate that Jesus officially selected Mary Magdalene to lead the church. While there is no solid evidence to support such claims, there are numerous references to women doing important mission work and helping to establish congregations of believers during the first and second centuries. As the church grew, women continued to be powerful witnesses to Jesus' message, often despite the sinfulness of a male-dominated culture. Examples through the centuries include: Perpetua, Monica, Clare, Teresa of Avila, Julian of Norwich, Catherine of Sienna, Katherina von Bora, Susanna Wesley, Catherine Booth, Mother Teresa, and, in present-day culture, Vonette Bright and Anne Graham Lotz.

female leadership in the Old Testament Historically, nations and governments have been led by male rulers, so it's not surprising that many Old Testament leaders were male. Nonetheless, the biblical cast is filled with brilliantly talented women who played prominent roles in Israel's history. Consider the following examples of female leadership:

- Esther, a courageous woman who, at the risk of her own life, beseeched and ensured the Persian king's mercy upon her people (Esther 1–10)
- Ruth, who was faithful to her family (and became part of Christ's lineage) after her husband had died and she was living in a foreign land (Ruth 1–4)
- Deborah, a judge and commander before Israel had kings (Judges 4)

Proverbs 31 affirms the greatness of women, praising their ability to sustain excellence in leadership, commerce, marriage, and mothering.

female leadership in the New Testament One of the most remarkable elevations of females and their importance to Israel's history is found in the genealogy of Jesus (Matt. 1:1–16). While lineage was traditionally traced back through each generation on the father's side, five women are highlighted: Tamar, Rahab, Ruth, Bathsheba, and Mary, mother of Jesus.

Throughout his ministry Jesus was surrounded by female followers, considered worthy of enjoying his company and hearing his teachings alongside his male disciples. Women funded Jesus' itinerant ministry (Luke 8), and women were predominantly present at his crucifixion. The women who went to the tomb to anoint Jesus' body with spices were chosen to confirm the resurrection, Christianity's most historically important event; in first-century culture, women had not been perceived as sufficiently credible to be witnesses in court, yet the Bible stakes its case on a female eyewitness account.

Also, Acts shows that women had substantial roles in ministry, and Paul praises the contributions of women such as Phoebe (Rom. 16:1).

Festal Letter See Athanasius of Alexandria.

Fibonacci sequence, The In the thirteenth century, mathematician Fibonacci (Leonardo Pisano) wondered (in *Liber Abaca*): "How many pairs of rabbits will be produced in a year, beginning with a single pair, if in every month each pair bears a new pair which becomes productive from the second month on?" The sequence of numbers, following Fibonacci's formula, runs thusly: 1, 1, 2, 3, 5, 8, 13, 21, 34, 55, 89, 144, 233, etc., and each number is equal to the sum of the two preceding it. (Rabbits would proliferate prodigiously, according to this hypothetical!) What's amazing about the formula's recursive sequence is that it's actually found throughout the natural world: the growth patterns of plants and the spirals of nautilus shells (for example) follow this mathematical sequence. Fibonacci's discovery is one of many suggestive evidences that the universe is structured in accord with mathematical principles (*DVC*, 60).

five-petal rose See rose as symbol.

fleur-de-lis *The Da Vinci Code* (111, 114) asserts that this is said to be the symbol for the Priory of Sion and is part of the code that connects the secret society with Leonardo da Vinci. The *fleur-de-lis,* the origin of which remains unknown, is an ancient symbol that can be found in many cultures, from the ancient Assyrians to the French monarchy under the reign of Phillippe-Auguste. In Christian traditions, the *fleur-de-lis* is sometimes used to represent the three persons of the Trinity or the Virgin Mary.

form criticism Subfield of biblical studies; the study of a story's history, with the goal of determining the original form and meaning. Rudolf Bultmann (d. 1976), a German New Testament scholar, used form criticism to "demythologize" biblical narratives—that is, to remove what he decided were "miraculous legends" and then look for the "kernels of truth" that originally inspired them. For the biblical authors, the historical veracity of miraculous events was just as important as the truths that inspired the writing of the stories (e.g., see 1 Cor. 15:12–20). See also deconstructionism; exegesis; redaction criticism; textual criticism.

Freemasonry The Freemasons are a worldwide fraternal order emphasizing deistic metaphysics and military-style morality. The fraternity's symbol—a square and a compass—indicates its original efforts to connect with the medieval stonemasons' guild. The era between 1580 and 1750 brought an increased interest in secret societies, hidden knowledge, and even witch-craft; one cause may have been the Protestant Reformation and the attacks on the Roman Catholic Church.

Modern Freemasons modeled their associations on the traditions and patterns of the Scottish Masons: adopting a patron, developing rituals and symbols, building lodges for their meetings. When educated men joined operative guilds, hoping to discover mystical knowledge or secrets long kept from the public, their subsequent beliefs and their interests in sci-ence and alchemy transformed the working-class nature of skill-based guilds to that of secret societies containing symbolism and rituals un-related to craftsmanship. (Speculative [in contrast to operative] masons belong to societies made up of people from different occupations, regard-less of skill or ability.)

In the sixteenth century, William Shaw wrote down the first lists of Masonic statutes and codes. In the tradition of the Roman *collegiums,* he also chose a patron for the guild: William Sinclair, a descendant of the mason who built Rosslyn Chapel. By the eighteenth century, Freemasons were concentrated in England, France, and Germany (*DVC,* 203).

Friday, October 13, 1307 According to Dan Brown (*DVC,* 159–60), this date is the origin for the unlucky "Friday the thirteenth," though there are many theories on that designation's origin. On October 13, 1307, France's King Philip IV ordered the abrupt arrest of all the Knights Tem-plar, which had accrued considerable monies and lands in two centuries. Philip accused the Templars of various forms of sacrilege, and since they were a tightly disciplined secret order, they had difficulty disclosing their true activities. Pope Clement V vehemently protested the king's actions, and he suspended the bishops and inquisitors who helped interrogate and torture the Knights, but by 1312 he had become persuaded that the order was sufficiently nefarious and corrupt to suppress it. Dan Brown's account eliminates Philip's role in the process, singularly blaming the pope, who in fact had initially tried valiantly to protect the order. See also Clement V, Pope; Knights Templar; Philip IV, King.

Fulk of Chartres/Fulcher de Chartres French knight who participated in the First Crusade; wrote *A History of the Expedition to Jerusalem,* an inval-uable primary historical source. The authors of *Holy Blood, Holy Grail* see his "thunderous silence" (67) regarding the activities of the Knights Tem-plar as evidence of a conspiracy.

Gardner, Gerald The English "father of Wicca"; d. 1964; served as a government employee in the Far East between the World Wars and was profoundly impressed by certain native religions; retiring to England, he wrote a novel, *A Goddess Arrives* (1939), that celebrated the worship of Aphrodite in ancient Cyprus. During the 1940s he involved himself with the Fellowship of Crotona, an occult offshoot of Masonry established by the daughter of Annie Besant, a noted Theosophist fascinated with witchcraft. Gardner met Aleister Crowley in 1946; the two shared interests in paganism, goddess worship, and various other New Age elements. In the last decade of his life, he published *Witchcraft Today* and *The Meaning of Witchcraft*. See also Crowley, Aleister; Theosophy.

gargoyle From French *gargouille,* "throat," or Latin *gurgulio,* "swallow, gurgle"; any spout that diverts water from a roof. The term refers most frequently to a grotesque statue, the mouth of which normally serves as the drain-spout (*DVC,* 227).

Garlow, James L., and Peter Jones Authors of *Cracking Da Vinci's Code* (not to be confused with Simon Cox's *Cracking the Da Vinci Code*). See Jones, Peter.

genuflection The Latin phrase *genu flectere* means to "bend the knee"; done as an act of reverence in Catholic and Episcopal churches. Genuflection is an attitude of humility, a kneeling in submission as part of worship and prayer. Ambrose said: "The knee is made flexible by which the offence of the Lord is initiated, wrath appeased, grace called forth" (*Hexaem,* VI.ix). Alcuin explained: "By such posture of the body we show forth our humbleness of heart" (*De Parasceve*).

Gerard de Sede Author of *Les Templiers sont parmi nous* (*The Templars Are Among Us*, 1962), which first revealed information about the fictional Priory of Sion. Henry Lincoln, coauthor of *Holy Blood, Holy Grail*, read Gerard's book, eventually contacting him and then beginning an investigation into the secrets surrounding documents found in the village church at Rennes-le-Château. These documents supposedly protected an explosive truth hidden by the Roman Catholic Church; it is now known that his information was fabricated, but *The Da Vinci Code*'s popularity has reenergized the legend.

gnomon Greek term meaning "source of knowledge"; the part of a sundial that casts a shadow. Dan Brown presents the gnomon at Saint-Sulpice in Paris as "a pagan astronomical device" (*DVC*, 105). However, the gnomon is neither pagan nor Christian; the one at Saint-Sulpice was constructed to predict accurately the dates of Christmas and Easter.

gnosis Greek for "knowledge"; in Gnosticism, a direct experience of the divine that results in a new level of knowledge. Dan Brown says that men in ancient times achieved *gnosis* through a sexual ritual known as *Hieros Gamos* (*DVC*, 308); although such rituals probably occurred in some Gnostic cults, no reliable evidence suggests that these practices were widespread. Many ancient temples did include sex with temple prostitutes as part of worship. See also Gnosticism; *Hieros Gamos.*

Gnosticism From Greek *gnosis,* "knowledge"; religious movement that blended elements from pagan mythology, Greek philosophy, Judaism, and Christianity into a single paradigm in which devotees attempted to achieve *gnosis,* a special level of insight into the inner nature of the cosmos. Although many aspects of Gnosticism may be traced to pre-Christian followers of Plato, Gnosticism probably emerged within Christianity in the last half of the first century AD.

Until the mid-twentieth century, little was known about Gnosticism outside the anti-Gnostic writings of the church fathers. The discovery of an ancient library of Gnostic texts near Nag Hammadi in Egypt revealed much more about their early theology and practices. Most Gnostics shared at least three beliefs.

First, the deity that created the universe was not the supreme and true

God. The creator—known among some Gnostics as "Ialtabaoth" or "the Demiurge"—was an evil deity who most Gnostics believed was the Old Testament God; they held that Jesus had been sent by a greater, higher deity.

Second, believing the physical universe was created by an evil deity, Gnostics viewed everything physical as evil. With rare exceptions, Gnostics viewed sexuality—and especially the woman's part in procreation—as disgusting and vile. The apostle Paul was possibly describing early Gnostics when he wrote, "The Spirit clearly says that in later times some will abandon the faith. . . . They forbid people to marry" (1 Tim. 4:1, 3).

The Gnostic writings known as *Gospel of Eve* and *Gospel of Philip* do describe sexual practices among Gnostics, but it is unclear whether these descriptions were symbolic or if they describe actual, physical acts. If some Gnostics did participate in sexual rituals, their rationale seems to have been that since everything physical was already hopelessly evil, what they did with their bodies was of little consequence.

The Gnostics saw women as inferior and unworthy. According to the last verse of the *Gospel of Thomas,* when "Simon Peter said to Jesus, 'Let Mary leave us; women aren't worthy of life,' Jesus replied, 'I will lead her to become male, so she can become a living spirit like you males. For every woman who makes herself male will enter the kingdom of heaven.'"

Early Christians—recognizing that the Creator of the physical cosmos is both the God of Israel and the Father of Jesus Christ—rejected Gnosticism's negative view. The following are examples of Gnosticism's outlook on the material world, the physical body, womanhood, and sexuality.

- "Sexual intercourse continued due to the ruler of this world. He planted sexual desire in the woman that belonged to Adam. He produced through intercourse copies of the bodies, inspiring them with his spirit of opposition" (*Apocryphon of John*).
- "My mother [gave me falsehood], but [my] true [Mother] gave me life" (*Gospel of Thomas,* 101).
- "The one who is acquainted with father and mother will be called the son of a prostitute" (ibid., 105).
- Physical intercourse produces beasts, so Gnostic believers must "abandon bestiality" (*Book of Thomas the Contender,* 139:8–11, 28–29).

- "Annihilate the works which pertain to the woman [i.e., child-bearing] . . . so that they [the works of creation] may cease" (*Dialogue of the Savior,* 144:19–20).
- Femininity is "unclean" and is called Nature's "dark vagina" (*Zostrianos,* 131:5–8; see also *Testimony of Truth,* 68:6–8).
- Marriage is defilement; sexual intercourse, called the "intercourse of Darkness," will be destroyed at the end of time (*Gospel of Philip,* 82:4).
- The Gnostic believer must "flee from the insanity and fetters of female-ness, and embrace instead the salvation of maleness" (*Paraphrase of Shem,* 18:34–35; 27:2–3; 22:34).
- A curse on "you who love intimacy with womankind and polluted intercourse with it" (*Book of Thomas the Contender,* 144:9–10).
- "The body came from sexual desire, and sexual desire came from . . . matter" (*Authoritative Teaching,* 23:18–20).
- The soul came in "a contemptible body" (*Gospel of Philip,* 56:25).
- The physical world is a mistake or "an illusion" (*Treatise on The Resurrection,* 48:15).
- Jesus says: "I shall destroy [this] house [physical body], and no one will be able to rebuild it" (*Gospel of Thomas,* 71).
- "[The] body is bestial . . . [and] will perish" (*Book of Thomas the Contender,* 139:6–8).

Third, because they believed that everything physical was evil, Gnostics also held that Christ only *seemed* human, a belief known later as "Docetism" (from Greek *dokein,* "to seem"). According to *Coptic Apocalypse of Peter,* the man "whose hands and feet they nailed to the cross" was not actually Christ, because Christ did not have a body.

The earliest Christians knew, however, that Jesus Christ is not only fully God but also fully human. The apostle John was countering an early form of Docetism when he wrote, "This is how you can recognize the Spirit of God: Every spirit that acknowledges that Jesus Christ has come in the flesh is from God" (1 John 4:2; see also 2 John 7).

The Da Vinci Code makes several spurious claims about Gnosticism and the Nag Hammadi documents, including that these writings are the "earliest Christian records," that they represent "the original history of Christ," and that they speak "of Christ's ministry in very human terms" (*DVC,* 234, 245). It also implies that Gnostic groups highly valued women and participated in a sexual ritual known as *Hieros Gamos* (125–26, 308–10).

In truth, the *earliest* Gnostic texts were written around AD 150—a century after Paul's earliest letters and at least half a century after the latest canonical gospel; most known Gnostic writings stem from the second and third centuries. (Edwin Yamauchi's *Pre-Christian Gnosticism* demonstrates that full-fledged Gnosticism did not emerge until the second century, more than seventy years after Jesus walked the earth.) Far from representing "the original history of Christ," Gnostic writings represent a view of Jesus that emerged decades after his earthly ministry.

Furthermore, no Gnostic writing speaks "of Christ's ministry in very human terms"—most Gnostics didn't even believe he was a physical being. See also Docetism; Epiphanius of Salamis; heresy; *Hieros Gamos;* Marcion of Sinope; Nag Hammadi; orthodoxy.

Goddess in the Gospels, The The *Da Vinci Code*'s Leigh Teabing highlights this volume—a real-life writing by Margaret Starbird—as one of several by "historians" offering evidence that Jesus and Mary Magdalene were married and had a child (*DVC,* 254–55). A feminist writer with degrees in literature and German (not history) who left the Roman Catholic Church after reading *Holy Blood, Holy Grail,* Starbird promotes a goddess-centered religion and suggests that Mary Magdalene should be considered the equal of Jesus himself both as the divine wisdom (*sophia*) and as his bride.

goddess worship Religion that worships a female deity. *The Da Vinci Code*'s Robert Langdon says that Roman Emperor Constantine (r. 306–337) and church leadership eliminated Christian teachings that held feminine virtues as holy and representative of some of the Creator's qualities (*DVC,* 23, 125). Goddess worship holds feminine virtues as superior to male virtues, favoring a matriarchal church just as imbalanced and inequitable as the patriarchal structures most feminists despise.

Goddess worship pervaded much of the ancient world, except where Judeo-Christian faith prevailed. The past half millennium has seen a resurgence of cults favorable to goddesses, as illustrated by the Rosicrucians (c. 1600) and Freemasons (c. 1700). When Romanticism swept the West in the nineteenth century, celebrating love and the "ideal female," a thinker as influential as Goethe declared: "The Eternal Feminine draws us on high." Utopian socialists like Fourier and St. Simon felt this calling and celebrated the sacred feminine themes evident in Dan Brown's novel. (Nathaniel Hawthorne's wife, Sophia, lamented the "monstrous system" of the utopians and blamed it all on the French Revolution, when "people worshipped a naked woman as the Goddess of Reason.")

Johan Jacob Bachofen claimed that ancient peoples were blessed by matriarchal societies and goddess worship; theosophists like Madame Blavatski and Madame Tingley followed suit. Christian Science's Mary Baker Eddy taught her followers to address God as Father/Mother, and feminists such as Mary Daly (author of *Beyond God the Father*) have fully embraced a goddess version of spirituality. See also Freemasonry; Romanticism; Theosophy.

Godefroi de Bouillon d. 1100; also known as Godfrey of Bouillon. *The Da Vinci Code*'s Robert Langdon says that Godefroi was a French king, one of the only surviving Merovingians, leader of the First Crusade, and actual founder of the Priory of Sion; supposedly, it was Godefroi who ordered the Knights Templar to dig beneath the ruins of Solomon's temple to find proof of the descendants of Jesus and Mary Magdalene (*DVC*, 158, 258).

Godefroi de Bouillon was in fact not a French king but rather a duke who became the leader of an order of knights called Defender of the Holy Sepulchre. He was one of the first crusaders to enter Jerusalem on July 15, 1099. One week later, after Raymond IV of Toulouse refused to be named king of Jerusalem, Godefroi was elected in his place.

He refused the title, declaring that Jesus Christ is the only true king of Jerusalem, and instead claimed "Defender of the Holy Sepulchre." After imposing his power in several surrounding cities, Godefroi died, nineteen years before the founding of the Knights Templar. Muslim accounts say he was killed in battle; Christian chroniclers assert that he contracted a deadly illness while in Caesarea.

The Da Vinci Code asserts that Godefroi was "the possessor of a powerful secret" and that he founded "the Priory of Sion . . . in Jerusalem in 1099" to protect it (157). Supposedly, this secret included the knowledge that Jesus and Mary had a sexual relationship and that Godefroi himself was one of their descendants (257–58). Regarding this pseudo-historical reconstruction:

The Priory of Sion was founded not in the twelfth century by Godefroi but by Pierre Plantard in 1956 as part of an elaborate hoax. Plantard
forged documents in which he claimed that the Priory of Sion began during the First Crusade. The authors of *Holy Blood, Holy Grail* treated these
forgeries as actual historical sources, and *The Da Vinci Code* follows their
lead.

There is no reliable evidence that Jesus and Mary Magdalene had an
intimate relationship. The sources implying this—such as *Gospel of Mary
Magdalene* and *Gospel of Philip*—were written more than a century after
the time of Christ and do not reflect eyewitness testimony. See also Crusades; Dagobert II; *Gospel of Mary Magdalene; Gospel of Philip; Holy
Blood, Holy Grail;* Knights Templar; Mary Magdalene; Merovingian; Plantard, Pierre; Priory of Sion.

Godfrey of St. Omer Joined Hugh de Payens in requesting that Crusader
King Baldwin II authorize the establishment of the Knights Templar in
1118.

Golden Mean, Golden Ratio, Golden Section Mathematical terms; alternate names for the Divine Proportion. See Divine Proportion.

gospel Translation of Greek *euangellion,* "good message"; used in ancient
Greek literature to speak of important events; in typical Christian usage,
an account of Jesus Christ's life and ministry. See Gospels, canonical.

Gospel of Andrew, The Alternate title for *The Acts of Andrew.* See *Acts of
Andrew.*

Gospel of Barnabas, The Seventh-century (or later) Muslim writing; claims
to have been written by the biblical Barnabas; probably an attempt to
synthesize early Muslim beliefs with Christianity. Because the book mentions Muhammad by name, *Gospel of Barnabas* was written no earlier
than the seventh century, placing it more than six hundred years after
Barnabas. No early or medieval Christian writer considered this document
to have any authority for believers or any place among the canonical
Scriptures. See Gospels, canonical.

Gospel of Basilides, The Mid-second-century Gnostic writing, now lost;

mentioned by Irenaeus, Origen, and Jerome. No early Christian writer considered this document to have any authority for believers or any place among the canonical Scriptures. See also Gospels, canonical; Irenaeus of Lyons; Jerome; Origen of Alexandria.

Gospel of the Ebionites, The First- or second-century document; survives only in fragmented quotations scattered throughout early Christian writings; appears to have been a variation of *Gospel of the Hebrews,* edited to fit Ebionite theology. According to the church father Epiphanius, the Ebionites changed the text so that Jesus appeared to be a vegetarian and a created being, adopted by God at his baptism. No early Christian writer considered this document to have any authority for believers or any place among the canonical Scriptures. See also Bible; canon; church fathers; Ebionites; Epiphanius of Salamis; *Gospel of the Hebrews; Gospel of the Nazoreans.*

Gospel of the Egyptians, The Second-century document frequently confused with a later Gnostic writing known as *Coptic Gospel of the Egyptians;* presented as a dialogue between Jesus and a female disciple named Salome; encourages all believers to practice celibacy. When Salome asks, "How long will death prevail?" Jesus replies, "As long as women continue to bear children." This attitude contradicts the Jewish and Christian Scriptures' affirmation and blessing of sexual interaction between husband and wife (Prov. 5:18–19; Song 5:10–16; 7:1–13; Mark 10:6–8; 1 Cor. 7:3–5).

Although many second- and third-century Christians (especially in Egypt) were familiar with *Gospel of the Egyptians,* it was never considered to have any place among the canonical Scriptures. When Clement of Alexandria cited it in one of his second-century writings, he made clear that it wasn't authoritative: "We do not have this saying in the four Gospels that have been passed down to us but only in that according to the Egyptians" (*Stromata,* 3:13). Clement's words also demonstrate that the four canonical gospels had been established as the authoritative accounts of Christ's life at least by the second century. See also canon; Clement of Alexandria; Gnosticism.

Gospel of Eve, The Second- or third-century Gnostic writing (date probable), now lost. Quoted by Epiphanius of Salamis, who claimed that some Gnostics used its content to justify sexual immorality. The cited passage has many possible meanings: "I stood on a mountain and saw a tall man. . . . He said: I am you and you are me, and wherever you are, there I am, and I am sown in all things; and wherever you wish, you may gather me, but when you gather me, you gather yourself." In any case, *Gospel of Eve* was written at least a century after the time of Jesus and thus is not eyewitness testimony. No early Christian writer considered this document to have any authority for believers or any place among the canonical Scriptures. See Epiphanius of Salamis; Gnosticism.

Gospel of Gamaliel, The Fifth-century Christian writing; heavily influenced by *Acts of Pilate;* combines the supposed words of the Jewish rabbi Gamaliel with quotations from the gospel of John. Nothing in this work is heretical, but it was clearly written long after the apostolic era and is not likely to represent Gamaliel's authentic words. No early Christian writer considered this document to have any authority for believers or any place among the canonical Scriptures. See also *Acts of Pilate;* canon; Gospels, canonical.

Gospel of the Hebrews, The First-century Christian writing; original form uncertain; survives only in fragmented quotations scattered throughout early Christian writings. Some leaders intertwined the origins of *Gospel of the Hebrews* with the origins of the canonical gospel of Matthew. Even though Matthew was written in Greek, Epiphanius and Jerome seem to have believed he originally wrote in Aramaic and that *Gospel of the Hebrews* represented this original form. Papias testified that Matthew originally wrote "in Hebrew," a description that could fit a book written in Aramaic.

According to Eusebius, "Matthew . . . composed a Gospel about the Messiah. This Gospel was first published in Judea in Hebrew letters for the sake of circumcised believers. Afterward, the Gospel was rendered in Greek; the author of this rendering is uncertain. The Hebrew version has been preserved until the present day in the library at Caesarea, which Pamphilius so carefully gathered" (*Historia Ecclesiastica,* 4:22). As such, *Gospel of the Hebrews* was possibly translated into Greek—and perhaps merged with portions from Mark's gospel—to form the biblical gospel of Matthew.

If so, some portions of *Gospel of the Hebrews* were not included in Matthew's gospel, because there are quotations from it preserved by Clement, Origen, and Jerome not present in Matthew's gospel. If they were using an Aramaic copy of *Gospel of the Hebrews*, differences could stem out of their translations from Aramaic into Greek and Latin.

In the fourth century, Eusebius reported that a few Christians still used *Gospel of the Hebrews* (ibid., 2:25). Most likely, it passed out of usage because (1) it reported the same events as the canonical Gospels and (2) it was associated with the altered *Gospel of the Ebionites*. See also apostolic fathers; Aramaic; Bible; canon; church fathers; Epiphanius of Salamis; Gospels, canonical; *Gospel of the Ebionites;* Greek; Hebrew; Latin.

Gospel of James, The See *Infancy Gospel of James.*

Gospel of Judas, The Late-second-century Gnostic writing; alleged account of Christ's life, used by members of a Gnostic sect known as the Cainites. Only one copy has been located, in which large portions are missing. According to Irenaeus, *Gospel of Judas* presented Judas Iscariot as the hero of the Jesus story. No early Christian writer considered this document to have any authority for believers or any place among the canonical Scriptures. See apostle; Gospels, canonical; Irenaeus of Lyons.

Gospel of Mary, The Early-third-century Gnostic writing; Coptic text found in 1945 at Nag Hammadi; the two small extant fragments are translations of earlier Greek texts; words and phrases are missing. Neopaganists have heavily quoted lines from these few fragments as proof that Mary Magdalene was "the favored disciple"; however, although this document is frequently called *Gospel of Mary Magdalene,* the text never clearly indicates *which* Mary is the central character—she could be any of the seven New Testament disciples named "Mary."

One line says that Jesus "loved [Mary] more" than the other disciples, a statement *The Da Vinci Code* uses to imply that Mary had experienced a sexual relationship with him (247–48). In context, however, the disciples are arguing about the possibility that Jesus may have granted Mary a greater knowledge of his teachings than given to them. Although they eventually seem to accept her words about Jesus, *Gospel of Mary* still maintains a negative view of women; at one point she declares, "Let us praise Christ's greatness! He has prepared us all by making us men."

Dan Brown also implies that *Gospel of Mary* is "a gospel . . . in Magdalene's words" (247). The document's style, however, indicates that it was most likely written a century or more after the death of Mary Magdalene. No early Christian writer considered this document to have any authority for believers or any place among the canonical Scriptures. See Gnosticism; Mary Magdalene; Nag Hammadi.

Gospel of Matthias, The   Early-second-century document, now lost, known to many early believers; tells of Matthias's supposed imprisonment by cannibals, from whom he was rescued by Andrew. This text seems to have passed out of Christian usage because (1) no clear evidence suggested that the apostle Matthias actually wrote it and (2) it was used by a heretical sect known as "the Nazarenes" (another name for the Ebionites; "the Nazarenes" are not to be confused with present-day Nazarenes or Church of the Nazarene). While Gnostics embraced it, Origen and Eusebius dismissed it as heretical. *Gospel of Matthias* may be related to the document now known as *Traditions of Matthias* (or the *Oxyrhynchus 840 Gospel*).

As a historical figure, Matthias was one of the seventy whom Jesus sent on a preaching mission. When the apostles selected the successor of Judas Iscariot, Matthias was designated. Little else is known about him: some say he went to Ethiopia, where he was martyred; others that he was stoned to death in Jerusalem. See also apostle; Ebionites; *Gospel, Oxyrhynchus 840*.

Gospel of the Nazoreans, The   Also known as *Gospel of the Nazarenes;* most likely an alternate title for *Gospel of the Hebrews;* used by early writers such as Clement of Alexandria, Origen, Cyril of Jerusalem, and Jerome. See *Gospel of the Hebrews*.

Gospel of Nicodemus, The   Alternate title for *The Acts of Pilate*. See *Acts of Pilate*.

Gospel, Oxyrhynchus 840   Third-century (or earlier) writing; not actually a gospel, but a tiny papyrus fragment from an unknown source; describes a confrontation in the temple between Jesus and the Pharisees; its events do not contradict the canonical Gospels and seem to represent an expansion of the events described in Mark 7:1–23. "Oxyrhynchus" comes from the Egyptian village where the document was found. See also Gospels, canonical; Pharisees.

Gospel of Paul, The Alternate title for *The Acts of Paul.* See *Acts of Paul.*

Gospel of Perfection, The Lost Gnostic writing, perhaps identical to *The Gospel of Eve.* See *Gospel of Eve.*

Gospel of Peter, The Second-century docetic writing; Serapion of Antioch quickly discovered that it had been "falsely written under [the apostle's] name"; he even borrowed a copy of "this very gospel . . . from the successors of its authors." Although familiar to many early Christians, this text was never considered to have a place among the canonical Scriptures, probably because (1) it could not be clearly connected to an apostle and (2) some passages suggest that Jesus may not have been fully human: the suffering Jesus "remained silent, as if he felt no pain," and, when he died, he was simply "taken up." See also canon; Docetism; Gnosticism.

Gospel of Philip, The Late-third-century Gnostic writing; one copy found at Nag Hammadi; not actually a gospel, but a collection of brief excerpts from other Gnostic writings; summarizes the views of followers of Gnostic leader Valentinus. Unlike many Gnostic documents, *Gospel of Philip* does not claim to have been written by an apostle; the book is called by his name simply because he is the only apostle mentioned in it.

   The Da Vinci Code presents *Gospel of Philip* as primary proof that Jesus had a sexual relationship with Mary Magdalene. According to one character, it includes these words: "The companion of the Saviour is Mary Magdalene. Christ loved her more than all the disciples and used to kiss her often on her mouth." To this Dan Brown adds, "Any Aramaic scholar will tell you, the word *companion,* in those days, literally meant *spouse*" (246).

   The words "on her mouth" do not appear in the original text; however, *Gospel of Philip* does include sentences similar to the rest of the quotation above. This does not necessarily imply a marital or sexual relationship; kissing was—and continues to be—an accepted greeting in Middle Eastern cultures. Furthermore, the word translated *companion* does *not* imply that Mary was Jesus' spouse. (See "companion," Aramaic word for.)

Most important, even if *Gospel of Philip* did claim Jesus and Mary were married, its testimony would still be questionable. The book's origins can be traced to the Gnostic community that arose several years after the death of Valentinus (c. 160); written more than a century after Jesus walked the earth, the book cannot represent eyewitness testimony about him. Some of the brief excerpts found in *Gospel of Philip* may stem from the early second century; however, the date of the final form of the book is closer to the late 200s.

It is also from this document that Dan Brown apparently derives some of his description of *Hieros Gamos; Gospel of Philip* mentions a "mirrored bridal chamber" where persons can receive "a male power or a female power," yet it's uncertain whether these phrases refer to a sexual act or to a spiritual union between humanity and the divine. If the phrase does refer to a sexual act, *Gospel of Philip* shows that it's not a frenzied group ritual (as *The Da Vinci Code* describes) but a physical union shared between husband and wife: "If a marriage is open to the public, it has become prostitution, and the bride plays the harlot not simply when she is impregnated by another man but even if she . . . is seen by another man." No early Christian writer considered this document to have any authority for believers or any place among the canonical Scriptures. See also "companion," Aramaic word for; Gnosticism; *Hieros Gamos;* Nag Hammadi; Valentinus.

Gospel of the Savior, The Alternate title for *The Vision of the Savior*. See *Vision of the Savior*.

Gospel of Thomas, The Mid- to late-second-century Gnostic writing (long after the apostle Thomas's death); collection of sayings attributed to Jesus. Many are similar to statements found in the Synoptic Gospels (Matthew, Mark and Luke); a few may represent an early form of Gnosticism. Certainly, *Gospel of Thomas* exhibits a negative view of women not found in the New Testament. According to *Gospel of Thomas*, "every woman who makes herself male will enter the kingdom of heaven." No early Christian writer considered this document to have any authority for believers or any place among the canonical Scriptures, probably because its theology was questionable and because it could not be clearly connected to Thomas.

See also canon; Gospels, canonical; Nag Hammadi; Synoptic Gospels.

Gospel of Truth, The   Late-second-century Gnostic writing, unearthed at
Nag Hammadi; possibly also called *The Gospel of Valentinus;* according to
Irenaeus, a disciple of Valentinus wrote it; a retelling of the creation story
and the life of Jesus. The theology fits closely with what's known about
Valentinus, and many scholars have accepted Irenaeus's ascription. No
early Christian writer considered this document to have any authority for
believers or any place among the canonical Scriptures. See also Gnosticism; Irenaeus of Lyons; Nag Hammadi; Valentinus.

Gospels, canonical   Four writings—Matthew, Mark, Luke, and John—
accepted by Christians as the authoritative records of the first-century life
and ministry of Jesus.

The Da Vinci Code says "more than 80" gospels were considered for
inclusion in the Bible, and that the four canonical Gospels were selected
and edited by Emperor Constantine in the fourth century (231–34). The
historical evidence does not, however, support this claim (see Papias of
Hierapolis on the origins of the first two gospels).

Irenaeus, Tertullian, and Eusebius testify that the apostle Paul used
the gospel of Luke, indicating that Luke was accepted as authoritative no
later than Paul's death in AD 65.

Irenaeus also testifies that John's gospel was written to combat the
Gnostic teachings of Cerinthus, active in the late first century. A fragment
of John's gospel, found in Egypt and known as Rylands Papyrus P52, has
been dated in the early second century, suggesting that it was in wide cir-
culation by 100.

No later than the late first century, Christians throughout the world
accepted Matthew, Mark, Luke, and John as the reliable and authoritative
accounts of Jesus' life and ministry. This attitude was so widespread that,
when Irenaeus wrote *Against Heresies* in the second century, he com-
mented, "Since there are four quarters of the earth . . . it is fitting that
the church should have four pillars . . . the four Gospels." See also Bible;
canon; Eusebius of Caesarea; *Gospel of the Hebrews;* Irenaeus of Lyons;
Papias of Hierapolis; Tertullian of Carthage.

Gothic architecture   Dan Brown contends that the Knights Templar used

Gothic architecture to maintain the secret of the "sacred feminine"; he also alleges that their structures were built to represent intimate female anatomy. However, the Templars were not responsible for the construction of the cathedrals of their era.

Grand Occident, The In nineteenth-century France, when Freemasons led the republic, anti-Semitic groups feared the possible power of Judeo-Masonic conspiracies. Out of the anti-Masonic groups organized, one was the "Grand Occident." In the twentieth century, Pierre Plantard, an anti-Semite and the main figure behind the Priory of Sion farce, believed in the Grand Occident's ideas and tried to form an anti-Semitic group himself, then was imprisoned for failing to register it with the government. See Alpha Galates; Freemasonry; Plantard, Pierre.

Greco-Roman world, The Historical term referring to the cultures of Greece and Rome that dominated the Mediterranean world from the third century BC into the fifth century AD. See also Hellenism.

Greek Language derived from the ancient Mycenaean civilizations. (Mycenaean is the term applied to the art and culture of Greece from c. 1600 to 1100 BC.) After the conquests of Alexander the Great, the Greek dialect known as *Koine* ("common") was spoken throughout southern Europe, northern Africa, southwestern Asia, and the Middle East. *Koine* was the language of the New Testament and of the earliest Christian writings. See also Alexander the Great; Hellenism; Hellenization.

guild Denotes an association of workers who share the same skills and interests. The origin of the word *guild* comes from the same root as the German word *gelt,* which means "money." In the Middle Ages, the guild's most important function was to ensure each member received a proper Christian burial; as time progressed, skill competency became an important guild function, and a system of apprentices and teachers/masters developed. Apprentices would often take oaths of secrecy to protect the guild's teachings and swore loyalty to the other members. Many guilds adopted saints, and many also developed secret systems of symbols and passwords in order to protect the skill levels of their crafts (*DVC,* 436). See also Freemasonry.

Guillaume de Tyre Also known as William of Tyre; d. c. 1190; named Archbishop of Tyre in the newly established Crusader state; well-educated in classical literature; wrote *History of Jerusalem*, which deals with the First Crusade and the establishment of the Knights Templar. An accomplished traveler, Guillaume wrote an account of the Third Lateran Council, which he attended in 1179, and also a history of the Middle East (now largely lost); he helped to influence the launching of the Second Crusade.

H

Hammer Codex See *Codex Leicester.*

Hanegraaff, Hank, and Paul L. Maier Authors of *The Da Vinci Code, Fact or Fiction?*

Havah Hebrew for "Eve," from the verb meaning "live." According to Dan Brown, "The Jewish tetragrammaton YHWH—the sacred name of God—in fact derived from Jehovah, an androgynous physical union between the masculine *Jah* and the pre-Hebraic name for Eve, *Havah*" (*DVC,* 309). *YHWH,* far from being a compound of *Jah* and *Havah,* is a noun derived from the Hebrew *hayah* ("to be"); it was a variation of this term—*ehyeh* ("I Am")—that God spoke to Moses through the burning bush (Ex. 3:4). See also *Adonai; Jah; Jehovah;* Tetragrammaton; *YHWH.*

Hebrew Ancient Semitic language, still spoken in Israel. Known as *Lashon Ha-Kodesh* ("the Sacred Language") by the Jewish people, Hebrew is the primary language of the Old Testament. In its earliest written form, Hebrew had no vowels; "vowel points"—small symbols to aid in pronunciation—were added later. See also Aramaic.

Hellenism From Greek *hellene,* "Greek." The far-reaching, permeating culture that emerged following the military campaigns of Alexander the Great, when Greek became the dominant language of people of other ethnic heritage. See also Alexander the Great; Greek.

Hellenization From Greek *hellene,* "Greek." The process, initiated by the accomplishments of Alexander the Great and carried on by his successors, through which non-Greek peoples embraced Hellenic language and culture to form the Greco-Roman empire that dominated the ancient world for more than seven hundred years (from the third century BC into the fifth century AD). See also Alexander the Great; Greek; Latin.

Heraclius Roman Catholic archbishop and Latin Patriarch of Jerusalem; d. 1191. After the First Crusade (1095–1099), French crusaders established "the Kingdom of Jerusalem" in southern Palestine, whose Roman Catholic churches were overseen by an archbishop (known as the Latin Patriarch of Jerusalem); Heraclius was the twelfth of these. In 1184–1185 he traveled to Europe, seeking a new ruler for the kingdom; while in London, he consecrated the Temple Church, English headquarters of the Knights Templar (*DVC*, 343). After he returned, Jerusalem fell to the Muslim general Saladin; when the seaport Acre became the new crusader capital, Heraclius died there during Saladin's siege. See also Crusades; Knights Templar.

heresiologist A student of heresies, such as Irenaeus or Hippolytus in the ancient church. Thinkers engaged in the ministry of "apologetics"—that is, "defending the faith"—frequently focus on this endeavor, seeking to clarify orthodoxy ("right belief") while demonstrating how it has historically congealed and solidified through the process of refuting various heresies. In *The Da Vinci Code*, heretics admonished or rebuked by the church are frequently embraced as oppressed victims of tyranny. See also orthodoxy.

heresy From Greek *haireisthai*, "to choose for oneself," and *hairesis*, "choice"; in Christian theology, a belief that deviates from the essential message of Jesus Christ proclaimed by the apostles and recorded in the Scriptures; such belief represents an individual's decision to choose his or her own way rather than embracing "the faith that was once for all entrusted to the saints" (Jude 3). Dan Brown summarizes the history of the word *heresy* this way: Fourth-century Emperor Constantine "financed a new bible, which omitted those gospels that spoke of Christ's *human* traits. . . . Anyone who chose the forbidden gospels over Constantine's version was deemed a heretic. The word *heretic* derives from that moment in history. The Latin word *haereticus* means 'choice.' Those who 'chose' the original history of Christ [meaning, the canonical Gospels don't contain the original history] were the world's first *heretics*" (*DVC*, 234). Brown's claims are patently false:

- The word *heretic* was in common usage more than a century *before* Constantine. Forms of the term *heresy* appear in the first-century New Testament writings (1 Cor. 11:19; Gal. 5:20; 2 Peter 2:1). The word gained wide usage among Christians in the second century, after Irenaeus wrote *Against Heresies;* he contrasted beliefs found in the Scriptures—which he called *orthodoxy*—with self-chosen beliefs, which he dubbed *heresies.*

- The apostolic authors and the church fathers used the word *heresy* to describe beliefs deviating from the most ancient records about Jesus—precisely the opposite of Brown's allegation. Even when they did not use the word *heresy,* protecting the message of Jesus was clearly foremost in their minds: Paul repeatedly referred to truths "passed down" from Jesus and "entrusted" to Christians (Rom. 6:17; 1 Cor. 11:2, 23; 15:3). John specifically stated that if someone chose certain beliefs about Jesus that deviated from the original message, his or her faith was not authentic (1 John 2:22–24; 4:1–3; 2 John 7). See also apostle; Bauer, Walter; church fathers; Constantine the Great; heterodoxy; Irenaeus of Lyons; Julian the Apostate; orthodoxy.

hermaphrodite An organism with both male and female sex organs. Rarely found among vertebrates, there are nevertheless a few human beings so biologically identified. Sometimes "hermaphrodite" is ascribed to persons ambiguous about their sexual identity. *The Da Vinci Code* makes much of the notion that the *Mona Lisa* is androgynous, suggesting (to Dan Brown) the hermaphrodite fusion of Isis and Amon, ancient Egyptian deities (*DVC,* 120–21). See Amon; androgyny; Isis; *Mona Lisa.*

hermeneutics From Greek *hermeneuein,* "to translate" or "to interpret." Theological term, describing the methods used to interpret biblical and theological texts.

Herod's temple See temple, Herod's.

heterodoxy From Greek *heterodoxa,* "of another glory" or "of another opinion." Alternate term for "heresy"; erroneous teaching. See heresy; orthodoxy.

hidden documents According to *The Da Vinci Code,* the Priory of Sion created the Knights Templar to recover "a stash of hidden documents buried beneath the ruins of Herod's temple" (*DVC,* 158); these documents supposedly provided proof that Jesus and Mary Magdalene had been married. Although some Knights evidently explored the area beneath the Temple Mount in the early 1100s, they were likely seeking relics and treasures, not documents. (In 1867, British engineers excavating a series of tunnels beneath the Mount found a Templar cross, a spur, a broken lance, and part of a sword.) No reliable evidence suggests that the Templars found *any* documents—much less documents about Jesus Christ hidden beneath the ruins of a Jewish holy place. See Godefroi de Bouillon; Holy of Holies; Knights Templar; Priory of Sion; purist documents; temple, Herod's.

hierodules Slaves or dancers, generally child prostitutes, serving in religiously sanctioned temples; endemic in India until the British decreed "cult prostitution" illegal in 1860. Dan Brown's allegations (*DVC,* 309) regarding temple prostitution in ancient Judaism—in the Holy of Holies, no less—ignores the fact that the Israelites sought to stamp out this very activity (part of Baal worship and its associated fertility rituals) in the Promised Land. See Holy of Holies; temple, Solomon's.

Hieros Gamos Greek for "Temple Marriage" or "Sacred Union"; sexual ritual described in *The Da Vinci Code,* which says a "man could achieve a climactic instant when his mind went totally blank and he could see God" (*DVC,* 309); also claims this continued among Jews and Christians, even in the Jewish temple (309), until the established church engaged in a "brutal crusade to 'reeducate' the pagan and feminine worshiping religions" (125). Such claims are false, unfounded, and absurd. While some in nearly every religion have attempted to experience God through peculiar ceremonies, including sexual rituals,

- the Old Testament specifically stated God's displeasure with anyone who tried to provide deeper experiences of the divine through ritualistic sex, referring to them as cult or shrine prostitutes (Deut. 23:17).
- When the Israelites did allow ritualistic sex around their temple (1 Kings 14:24), righteous kings such as Josiah destroyed the houses

used for these ceremonies (2 Kings 23:7; 2 Chronicles 34:33; cf. 1 Kings 15:12; 22:46).

First-century rumors accused Christians of engaging in ritualistic sex during the Lord's Supper. According to one tale preserved by Minucius Felix, "After much feasting . . . they involve themselves . . . in unions of abominable lust." Partly because of such charges, Roman governors were suspicious of them; however, when Pliny, governor of Bithynia (northwest Asia Minor, in present-day Turkey) investigated Christian worship, here's what he discovered as standard: "On a fixed day, they . . . gather before daylight and sing a hymn to Christ as God. They bind themselves to one another as with an oath. . . . After this, they disperse and come together again to partake of ordinary food."

The Gospel of Philip, a document from a sect that tried to blend Christian faith with Greek mystery cults, does describe a ceremony of "sacred union," but this text probably dates from the late third century—more than two hundred years after Christianity's beginnings. See also *Gospel of Philip;* Holy of Holies; temple, Solomon's.

Hippolytus Christian theologian; d. 235; preserved an early form of the Apostles' Creed in his *Apostolic Tradition;* also wrote a major work against Gnosticism, *Refutation of All Heresies.* According to Hippolytus, when new believers received baptism, "the one baptizing . . . shall ask, 'Do you believe in Jesus Christ, the Son of God, who was born of the Holy Spirit and the Virgin Mary, who was crucified under Pontius Pilate, and died, and rose on the third day living from the dead, and ascended into heaven, and sat down at the right hand of the Father, the one coming to judge the living and the dead?'" This tradition demonstrates that certain beliefs about Christ were well-established among believers at least as early as the third century, and the reference to Jesus as "Son of God . . . born of the Holy Spirit" highlights the absurdity of Dan Brown's claim that Christians did not recognize Jesus as God's Son until 325, (*DVC,* 233). See also Council of Nicaea; Jesus as Son of God.

Holy Blood, Holy Grail Book coauthored by Michael Baigent, Richard Leigh, and Henry Lincoln (1982), suggesting that documents discovered by French priest Bérenger Saunière in 1885 were the first of many clues that could prove Mary Magdalene and her offspring had fled to France after the capture of Jesus, her husband and the father to her child/children. In this theory the Holy Grail is both a receptacle for the blood of Jesus (Mary's womb) and the royal bloodline of Jesus that exists even today.

The writers provide a fascinating view of history, involving much secrecy, conspiracy, and deception in order to protect the grail's real meaning. *The Da Vinci Code* refers to this volume as the breakthrough book in exposing this mystery to the public (*DVC,* 253), but in *Holy Blood, Holy Grail*'s introduction, Lincoln acknowledges that its style is like that of a novel and that their approach to gathering information and developing hypotheses was in this style as well. In their conclusion, the writers present their findings only as theory and admit that much of the evidence provided for the reader is based on rumors, gossip, legends, and cultural traditions. See also Baigent, Michael.

Holy Grail, The Many today consider the Holy Grail to be the cup used by Jesus and his disciples during the Last Supper; some also believe Joseph of Arimathea held the cup to catch the blood from Jesus' side as he died.

In 1170, Frenchman Chretien de Troyes wrote a poem called *Perceval,* seemingly based on Celtic myths, in which the grail is simply a jeweled dish. As the story was retold and rewritten, a distinctive theme emerged. Before the twelfth century, there were no legends about the grail; by the thirteenth century the tale had become intertwined with Arthurian legends, the characters from Chretien's story developed into supposed historical figures from the Gospels, and the grail had become the Holy Grail.

The Da Vinci Code's Leigh Teabing says that the French word for "Holy Grail," *Sangreal,* is actually an incorrect rendering of the words *Sang Real,* which would mean "Royal Blood." This idea is based on a suggestion made in *Holy Blood, Holy Grail* that at one point the word may have been miscopied and divided in the wrong place; the writers admit this is an unlikely possibility.

The pieces begin to fall into place for *The Da Vinci Code* characters once they begin to consider ancient pagan symbols for females (chalice) and males (blade). However, there is no historical evidence to connect the ancient chalice and the Holy Grail, since the grail's concept can only be traced back as far as the twelfth century (*DVC,* 162, 238, 250). See also chalice; *Holy Blood, Holy Grail.*

Holy of Holies, The Innermost chamber of the ancient Jewish tabernacle and temple, where the high priest sought atonement for the people's sins and where the Ark of the Covenant was kept. Dan Brown makes at least two incredible claims about the Holy of Holies:

- "Beneath the Holy of Holies, a sacred chamber where God Himself was believed to reside," the Knights Templar found proof that Jesus had children with Mary Magdalene (*DVC*, 159–60).
- "Early Jews believed that the Holy of Holies in Solomon's Temple housed not only God but also His powerful female equal, Shekinah" (*DVC*, 309).

First, the Jews did *not* believe that God lived in the Holy of Holies. When Solomon dedicated the temple, he said, "Will God really dwell on earth? The heavens, even the highest heaven, cannot contain you. How much less this temple I have built!" (1 Kings 8:27).

Second, although nine Knights may have explored the area beneath the Temple Mount in the early 1100s, no evidence suggests that they found any documents, and certainly not proof that Jesus and Mary Magdalene were married. Also questionable is how ancient Christian records would have ended up beneath the Jewish temple in the first place.

Third, *Shekhinah* [Hebrew spelling] was not God's "powerful female equal." The word, which doesn't appear in the Bible, means "the dwelling one," and it was used by later rabbis to describe how God lives among his people. See also hidden documents; Knights Templar; Shekhinah; temple, Herod's; temple, Solomon's.

Holy Roman Empire, The Loose confederation of German states that lasted—at least in theory—from the latter Middle Ages until the nineteenth century. Although its emperors claimed that the crowning of Charlemagne in 800 marked its beginning, the conglomeration that became the Holy Roman Empire emerged gradually after the Treaty of Verdun (843) divided the Frankish realm. At least as early as Otto I's crowning in 962, rulers viewed themselves as the royal heirs of the ancient Roman emperors. The title, though, is really a misnomer; as Voltaire once noted, the confederation of states was in truth "neither holy, nor Roman, nor an empire." In 1806 Napoleon Bonaparte defeated Emperor Francis II and reorganized the remnants into "the Confederation of the Rhine." See also Roman empire.

Holy See, The A "see" is the seat or residence of a bishop, the pastor of a cathedral city or designated region, who oversees or supervises his diocese. The "Holy See" generally refers to the seat of the Bishop of Rome, the pope of the Roman Catholic Church (*DVC,* 41).

Horus The word refers to various deities, but especially to Harseisis, the mythological son of Osirus and Isis; these three were involved in the cycle of death and rebirth. Isis was often portrayed holding the infant Horus as a suckling child, an imagery some have contended influenced later Christian iconography in portrayals of Mary and the baby Jesus. Another deity, Horus the Elder, was revered in Upper Egypt as the creator, the celestial being who gives being to all that is. "Horus" generally denoted the sky or sun as well; the living pharaoh was often regarded as a "living Horus."

House of David, The See David, House of.

Hugh de Payens Leader of the Order of the Poor Knights of Christ and the Temple of Solomon, otherwise known as the Knights Templar. When he and eight other French Knights vowed to protect traveling pilgrims, the king of Jerusalem granted them residence in the palace on the Temple Mount, originally the site of Solomon's temple, from whence these knights took their name. Hugh de Payens traveled throughout France, gaining recognition and financial support for the order.

Hugo, Victor Highly celebrated nineteenth-century French Romantic writer; two of his most enduring novels are *The Hunchback of Notre Dame* (1831) and *Les Misérables* (1862). Dan Brown's opening page states, "Fact: The Priory of Sion . . . is a real organization. In 1975 Paris's Bibliothèque Nationale discovered parchments . . . identifying members of the Priory of Sion, including . . . Victor Hugo" (*DVC,* 1, 88). In reality, the Priory was a farce created by Pierre Plantard. Archaeologist Bill Putnam succinctly said, "[The Priory of Sion] is the greatest hoax in my experience." (*Dateline,* NBC News, 4/13/05: Transcript 1762, 16.) See Plantard, Pierre; Priory of Sion.

iambic pentameter Among the types of poetry are:

- Iambic: a lightly stressed syllable followed by a heavily stressed syllable
- Anapestic: two light syllables followed by a stressed syllable
- Trochaic: a stressed syllable followed by a light syllable
- Dactylic: a stressed syllable followed by two light syllables

Iambic, probably the most common English form (beautifully illustrated in Shakespeare's sonnets), was widely used by the Greeks as well. In a line with ten syllables, alternating light and heavy syllables makes a meter line of five units or "feet"; meter lines are measured as *monometer* (one foot), *dimeter* (two feet), *trimeter* (three), *tetrameter* (four), *pentameter* (five—the one referenced in *The Da Vinci Code*), and so on.

Without offering evidence or demonstration, Dan Brown contends that iambic pentameter has mystical and pagan qualities. His characters also refer to English as a "pure" language (*DVC*, 303), a most unusual comment since English is the child of many languages and cultures. (German, for instance, would be a much more "pure" language, untouched by Latin or the "Romance languages," namely, French, Spanish, and Italian.)

iconology The study or analysis of icons (statues, images, or paintings) is a significant aspect of artistic and religious history (*DVC*, 8). In the early Middle Ages, the "iconoclastic controversy" rocked the church, especially its Greek-speaking Eastern section. After much discussion—and books written in their defense by theologians such as John of Damascus—the Seventh Ecumenical Council, meeting at Nicaea in 787, approved their use. For the Eastern Orthodox, says Nicholas Zernov, icons are "dynamic manifestations of man's spiritual power to redeem creation through beauty and art . . . pledges of the coming victory of a redeemed creation over the fallen one."

ideograms A combination of two Greek words—*idea* plus *writing*—an ideogram is a visual symbol, well-illustrated by Hittite, Egyptian, and Chinese characters. Unlike words made up of letters, an ideogram paints a picture that conveys an idea (*DVC,* 8).

Ignatius of Antioch Apostolic father; Christian teacher; d. 98/108; probably knew the apostles Peter and John personally. Ignatius was condemned to die for his faith, and on his way to the arena in Rome, he wrote seven letters that have survived to this day, providing valuable glimpses into the lives of early Christians. In his letter to the church at Magnesia, Ignatius reminded them that "there is only one God, and he has revealed himself through Jesus the Messiah, his Son and his Word." This is in obvious contrast to Dan Brown's *Da Vinci Code* claim that Christians did not view Jesus as divine until 325 (*DVC,* 233). See also apostolic fathers; Council of Nicaea.

illuminati The word means "the enlightened ones" (*DVC,* 8); groups of "illuminati" flourished in the fourteenth century as "The Brethren of the Free Spirit" as well as more recently in Bavaria, Spain, and France. Generally conspiratorial in their constitution and in their stance regarding the world; the histories of the Rosicrucians and Freemasons are replete with illuminati types. Dan Brown's *Angels and Demons* revolves around an illuminati plot against the Catholic Church. See also Freemasonry; Rosicrucians.

Infancy Gospel of James, The Apocryphal Christian writing, mid- or late-second century; an account, allegedly written by James the Just, of the life of Mary and the birth of Jesus. Mary is said to have remained a virgin throughout her life; the siblings of Jesus mentioned in the canonical Gospels were, according to this document, Joseph's children from a previous marriage (cf. Matt. 13:55; Mark 6:3). The writing style suggests a composition date at least a century after the death of James the Just, author of the epistle of James and half-brother (or stepbrother) of Jesus. Although Origen viewed *The Infancy Gospel of James* as an authentic account of

Mary's life, he did not treat it as part of the New Testament canon. In fact, no early Christian writer considered this document to have any authority for believers or any place among the canonical Scriptures. See also apocrypha; Gospels, canonical.

Infancy Gospel of Thomas, The Apocryphal Christian writing, mid-second century; an account, supposedly written by the apostle Thomas, of the childhood of Jesus; forms the source of many non-biblical legends regarding Jesus' early years. In this text, the boy Jesus repeatedly uses miraculous powers to bring life to a dozen clay birds, strike another child dead, and stretch a beam of wood. Although not necessarily heretical, this vision of Jesus differs radically from that of the canonical Gospels, where his miraculous powers are restrained and always focused on helping others. The author's style of writing and lack of knowledge about Jewish traditions suggest that the document was written long after Thomas's death; it cannot be connected to any eyewitness account of Jesus' life. No early Christian writer considered this document to have any authority for believers or any place among the canonical Scriptures. See also canon; *Gospel of Thomas;* Gospels, canonical.

infancy gospels Apocryphal books, such as *Pseudo-Matthew, James,* and *Thomas,* detailing events not mentioned in the canonical Gospels; the latter two have been the most popular. No early Christian writer considered the infancy gospels to have any authority for believers or any place among the canonical Scriptures. See also canon; Cullmann, Oscar; Gospels, canonical; *Infancy Gospel of James; Infancy Gospel of Thomas.*

Innocent II, Pope Roman Catholic pope (r. 1130–1143). According to *The Da Vinci Code,* Innocent II granted the Knights Templar "limitless power and declared them 'a law unto themselves'" because they had found proof that Jesus had married Mary Magdalene, and the pope wanted to keep them quiet (*DVC,* 159). In fact, Innocent II did not grant the Knights "limitless power"; he made them directly responsible to himself. The most probable purpose for this decree was to regulate them directly, not to silence them. See also Crusades; Knights Templar.

Innocent III, Pope Roman Catholic pope (r. 1198–1216); launched two crusades—the Fourth, against the Muslims, and the Albigensian, against the Cathari of southern France. See Albigensian Crusade; Cathari; Crusades.

Inquisition, The Established by Pope Lucius III in 1184, the Inquisition's general purpose was to provide an organized means for finding heretics, determining their guilt or innocence, and punishing those who unrepentantly propagated falsehood. Punishments ranged from undertaking a long pilgrimage or wearing a yellow cross for life to the confiscation of property, banishment, public recantation, long-term imprisonment, or even death. Death sentences were always carried out by the secular ruler; typically, Dominican monks served as the inquisitors, overseeing the suspected heretic's trial. In 1252, Pope Innocent IV allowed the Inquisition to torture suspected heretics to gain confessions of guilt.

The Da Vinci Code claims that, as part of the church's "deceitful and violent history," the Inquisition targeted "all female scholars, priestesses, gypsies, mystics, nature lovers, [and] herb gatherers," burning at the stake "an astounding five million women" (125). Although nothing can excuse the use of force and violence to uproot heresy, such claims represent egregious exaggerations (serious estimates range around fifty thousand). Frankly, one is too many, but the claim of "five million" is indefensible. Even with heresy convictions, death sentences were rare; burnings were ever rarer. Bernard Gui, a famous French inquisitor, found more than seven hundred guilty of heresy during his fifteen years as an inquisitor, and only forty-two—less than 6 percent of those convicted—were sentenced to death. Most were men. See *Malleus Maleficarum;* witch-hunts.

Irenaeus of Lyons Christian teacher; d. 202; leading pastor of Lugdunum, Gaul (now Lyons, France); influential theologian. The writings of Irenaeus were vital to the development of Christian thought in the second and third centuries; *Against Heresies* makes clear that at least as early as the second century, Christians recognized four and only four gospels: "Since there are four quarters of the earth . . . it is fitting that the church should have four pillars . . . the four Gospels" (3.1). Furthermore, this statement indubitably refutes Dan Brown's claim that "more than 80" gospels were considered for canonical inclusion and his even more bizarre claim that the four canonical gospels were selected and edited by

Constantine in the fourth century (*DVC,* 231–34). See also church
fathers; Constantine the Great; Gospels, canonical.

Ishtar/Astarte Phoenician goddess, prominent in Sidon, Carthage, and
Sicily—wherever the seafaring dwellers of ancient Palestine went. A fertility goddess, the sister and consort of Baal; rituals of worship included
prostitution cults and child sacrifice. Ishtar/Astarte antedates and seems to
have influenced the Greek reverence for Aphrodite.

Isis Apparently coming out of Nubia (located in today's southern Egypt),
the feminine archetype of creation, patron goddess of fertility and motherhood; "Isis" is a Greek corruption of the Egyptian word *Aset;* known as
"the Queen of Heaven." Says an ancient text: "In the beginning there was
Isis: Oldest of the Old . . . the Goddess from whom all Becoming of the
House of Life, Mistress of the Word of God. She was the Unique . . . a
wiser magician and more excellent than any other God."

Isis was the mythical mother of Horus and the wife and sister of Osiris, who was killed and dismembered by his brother Seth. Isis is said to
have reunited the pieces of Osiris and resurrected him as ruler of the
underworld. Osiris fathered Horus following his resurrection.

Isis is often depicted holding or suckling the infant Horus, which
many scholars believe influenced the traditional images of Mary and the
baby Jesus. While this connection is probably accurate, it was not the
biblical description of Jesus and Mary that the myth of Isis and Horus
influenced, but later, *post*-biblical traditions. See also Amon; Christology;
hermaphrodite; Horus; L'isa.

Jachin See *Boaz* and *Jachin*.

Jah German form of *Yah*, shortened form of the Hebrew *YHWH*. According to Dan Brown, "YHWH—the sacred name of God—is in fact derived from Jehovah, an androgynous physical union between the masculine *Jah* and the pre-Hebraic name for Eve, *Havah*" (*DVC*, 309). *YHWH*, far from being a compound of *Jah* and *Havah*, is derived from the Hebrew *hayah* ("to be"), and it was a variation of this term—*ehyeh* ("I Am")—by which God identified himself to Moses (Ex. 3:14). The Hebrews so revered God's name that they did not even speak it; instead, they substituted the word *Adonai* ("Lord") and used its vowels when they wrote *YHWH*. See also *Adonai; Jehovah,* Tetragrammaton; *YHWH*.

Jardins des Tuileries Highlighted in chapter 3 of *The Da Vinci Code;* the central park of Paris, running along the Seine River from the Louvre to the Concorde Square. Designed in 1664 by André le Nôtre (also responsible for the grounds surrounding Versailles), Jardins des Tuileries is spacious, filled with sidewalks, cafes, and pedestrians enjoying the grandeur of Paris's inner city.

Jehovah Because they viewed *YHWH*, God's personal name, as too holy to be spoken, the Jewish people substituted *Adonai* ("Lord") for it, even using the vowels from *Adonai* when writing *YHWH*. The word *Jehovah* emerged in the 1500s when a German translator combined the *Adonai* vowels with the *YHWH* consonants and came up with *Yahowah* (in German, *Jehovah*). *Jehovah* comes from *YHWH*, not the other way around. See *Adonai; havah; Jah;* Tetragrammaton; *YHWH*.

Jerome Church father; d. 420; also known as Eusebius Sophronius Hieronymus; translated the Bible from Greek and Hebrew into Latin. Because his Latin translation was in "common" or "vulgar" Latin, his rendering became known as the Vulgate, which remains the official Latin translation of the Roman Catholic Church. See also church fathers; *Gospel of the Hebrews.*

Jesus as mortal prophet According to *The Da Vinci Code,* Jesus was "a mortal prophet . . . a great and powerful man, but a man nonetheless" (233). The truth is, no one can prove that Jesus was divine, and no one can prove that Jesus was merely mortal: both beliefs require faith. It's possible, however, to examine the historical evidence for each. Ancient tradition and historical testimony maintain that many of the apostles who walked and talked with Jesus, the very ones who would have known whether he performed miracles and rose from the dead, experienced horrible deaths because they insisted, even when faced with persecution and torture, that Jesus was no mere mortal. It has been wisely said that while people may die for a lie, people will not typically die for something they know is a lie. As such, the martyrdoms of these eyewitnesses provide powerful support for Jesus as far more than a "mortal prophet." See apostle; Christology.

Jesus Seminar, The Controversial high-profile study group, founded in 1985 by biblical scholar Robert Funk, that seeks to determine what Jesus actually said and did. As they've approached the texts about Jesus, the majority of the Seminar's scholars have assumed that the miraculous elements of his life are fictional. Having started with this biased assumption, it's not surprising that the Jesus Seminar has concluded that Jesus was a human being, born of a human father, and that his resurrection was based on the visionary experiences of Peter, Paul, and Mary (Funk, *The Acts of Jesus,* 1998). The following respected biblical scholars (and others) have thoroughly debunked Jesus Seminar claims: Luke Timothy Johnson (*The Real Jesus*); Ben Witherington III (*The Jesus Quest*); N. T. Wright (*Jesus and the Victory of God*); William Lane Craig (*Will the Real Jesus Please Stand Up?*); Craig Blomberg (*The Historical Reliability of the Gospels*); J. P. Moreland and Michael J. Wilkins (*Jesus Under Fire: Modern Scholarship Reinvents the Historical Jesus*); Peter Jones (*Stolen Identity: The*

Conspiracy to Reinvent Jesus). See also Blomberg, Craig; Jones, Peter; Witherington, Ben, III.

Jesus as Son of God   Though *The Da Vinci Code* states "that almost everything our fathers taught us about Christ is false" (235), careful and analytical investigation reveals that almost everything this novel teaches us about Christ is false.

Dan Brown alleges that Jesus was not seen as divine until the fourth-century Council of Nicaea. However, Jesus was seen as divine long before the Council formally affirmed it (with a 316 to 2 vote that Brown calls "close").

In the Old Testament, "son of God" could refer to angelic beings, mighty human rulers, or the nation of Israel (Gen. 6:2–4; Ex. 4:22; Ps. 82:6; Hos. 11:1). Between the Testaments, "Son of God" pointed to the chosen nation and to the expected Messiah. Throughout the New Testament, Jesus is "the Son of God" (Matt. 4:3–6; 14:33; Mark 1:1; 3:11; Luke 4:41; 22:70; John 1:34; 20:31), referring to Jesus' divine origin and messianic identity (Luke 1:35).

All four New Testament gospels were written during the first century. *The Da Vinci Code* claim that Jesus was seen as merely human until the fourth century (233) is pure fiction. See Christology; Son of Man.

Jewish marriage   See marriage, Jewish.

Joan, Pope   According to some sources, a woman—disguised as a man—served as the leader of the Roman Catholic Church in the mid-ninth century, probably between 855 and 858; the earliest to report it was Martin von Trappau in his thirteenth-century *Chronicle of Popes and Emperors*. (The reference to this event in Anastasius Bibliothecarius's ninth-century *Lives of the Popes* is in a later-added footnote.) This account was widely accepted in the Middle Ages; the supposed woman pope was given the names "John VIII," "Agnes," and "Joan." The Tarot deck even includes a card entitled *La Papesse* (French, "The Female Pope"), perhaps inspired by Joan's legend. Protestant and Roman Catholic scholars have pointed out that if Pope Joan had really existed, there should be references to her papacy prior to the thirteenth century, as it would have been difficult (if not impossible) to erase all records about her that would have spanned four hundred years. See also Roman Catholic Church.

Jones, Peter Contemporary scholar, author, and lecturer on paganism, the New Testament, and *Da Vinci Code*-related themes; born in Liverpool, England; as a young student shared a desk for five years with classmate John Lennon of Beatles fame. After graduating from the University of Wales, Jones came stateside for a Master's from Gordon Divinity School and a doctorate from Princeton Theological Seminary. Moving to France, Jones taught at *La Faculté Libre de Théologie Réformée d'Aix-en-Provence* before returning to the U.S. to become a professor at Westminster Theological Seminary.

Jones has written *The Gnostic Empire Strikes Back* (1992), *Spirit Wars* (1997), *Gospel Truth/Pagan Lies* (1999), *Capturing the Pagan Mind*, (2003), and *Cracking Da Vinci's Code* (2004, with James L. Garlow). His most recent books are *Stolen Identity* (about contemporary attempts to revise the life of Jesus) and *The God of Sex;* he is also director of Christian Witness to a Pagan Planet, an organization dedicated to helping Christians understand neo-pagan spirituality.

Joseph of Arimathea All four canonical Gospels describe Joseph of Arimathea as a wealthy man who provided a tomb for Jesus' burial (Matt. 27:57; Mark 15:43; Luke 23:50–51; John 19:38). In the Middle Ages, several legends about Joseph emerged, claiming that he was the uncle of Jesus' mother, Mary, and that he had been the keeper of the Holy Grail. Dan Brown presents these conjectures as historical facts (*DVC,* 162, 255) with an added twist—that Mary Magdalene *was* the Holy Grail. However, there is no reliable supporting evidence; the only "evidences" are legends that arose hundreds of years after the events. See *Holy Blood, Holy Grail;* Holy Grail.

Josephus, Flavius (Joseph ben Matthias) Jewish historian; d. c. 100; priestly heritage and thorough education prepared him to be a member of the elite religious group called the Pharisees. Josephus was an historian— his writings were used by the early defenders of the Christian faith ("apologists")—an interpreter for the Roman emperor Titus, and a friend to Emperors Vespasian and Domitian. Some believed he gained this favor by providing intelligence to Vespasian during the First Jewish-Roman War

(66–73) and thus was guilty of treason. Regardless, his status earned him Roman citizenship, money, and freedom to devote his time to writing.

Some of Josephus's accounts are records of events he actually witnessed, and because he did not accept the Christian faith, his references to the early believers and their activities have been studied for centuries as "objective" historical accounts of what took place during the church's formative years.

Most widely known are his works *Jewish War* and *Antiquities of the Jews;* the former begins with the Maccabees and ends with the destruction of Herod's temple in AD 70; the latter includes a brief description of Jesus (known as *Testimonium Flavianum*). Unfortunately, this reference was altered in the early Middle Ages to the point that Josephus's original words on Jesus are uncertain. See also Maccabees; temple, Herod's.

Jubilees Late-second-century-BC Jewish writing; an expansion and reworking of materials from the canonical Genesis and Exodus. *Jubilees* is in the Old Testament canon of the Ethiopian Orthodox (Tewahedo) Church, but no early Christian writer considered it to have any authority for believers or any place among the canonical Scriptures. See canon.

Judea A mountainous, agricultural region south of Jerusalem and west of the Dead Sea. Following Solomon's demise, the kingdom of Israel was divided in two, with the southern section generally called Judea. By New Testament times, Judea referred only to southern Palestine, with Jerusalem always a part of it. King Herod was "King of Judea" when Jesus was born.

Judgment of Peter, The Alternate name, found in Rufinus of Aquileia's writings, for the first-century document *Didache.* See *Didache.*

Julian the Apostate Flavius Claudius Julian; son of Julius Constantius II, the half-brother of Constantine the Great; d. 363. At Constantine's death, a ruthless, savage power struggle resulted in the killing of most of his relatives. Julian survived, but memories of alleged "Christians" in his family butchering each other gravely disillusioned him. (Constantius II claimed to be a Christian.)

Julian was trained as a believer, but his tutor was likely a pagan; though he outwardly went through the Christian motions, he apparently developed strong anti-Christian views in adolescence. Sent to Gaul by his uncle, Emperor Constantius, Julian proved an admirable military leader and administrator. When Constantius was killed fighting in Persia, Julian succeeded him in 360 and quickly moved to reinstate paganism as the state religion, reopening pagan temples and approving animal sacrifices. Though he ridiculed Christians as "Galileans" and forbade their appointments to teaching positions, his persecution failed, and he only ruled two years. History's assigned title to him is revealing: a person who never practiced or is opposed to Christianity is known as a pagan, while one who once practiced but later renounced the faith is an apostate. Julian is reputed to have said—referring to Jesus—on his deathbed: "You have conquered, Galilean." See also Constantine the Great; heresy.

Judith Apocryphal book accepted into the Old Testament canons of the Roman Catholic and Eastern Orthodox Churches. See apocrypha; canon.

Justin Martyr Christian apologist; d. c. 165. A pagan philosopher, Justin converted to Christianity and eventually suffered martyrdom during the reign of Emperor Marcus Aurelius. Justin was one of the great Christian apologists (from Greek *apologia*, "defense"), scholars who defended the faith against pagans. The first twelve chapters of Justin's *Apology* ("defense," c. 150—some 175 years before Nicaea) seek to prove that Jesus is the Son of God, the Messiah predicted in the Jewish Scriptures. See also Jesus as Son of God.

Kabbalah The Hebrew word means "interpretation" or "hermeneutics" but is generally associated with a mystical Jewish school, given to esoteric speculation as to reasons for creation and commandments. By pondering Scripture minutely—every letter allegedly has special meaning—Kabbalahists delve into secrets regarding God and the cosmos and the "tree of life." Supposedly, for example, God taught special truths to angels, then to Adam, Abraham, and Moses; careful study is said to unveil hidden meanings to biblical passages, knowable only to an elite inner circle. There are resemblances between Kabbalah practitioners and the Gnosticism so basic to *The Da Vinci Code*'s message (98, 304).

Kellmeyer, Steven Author of *Fact and Fiction in The Da Vinci Code.*

keystone See *clef de voûte.*

Kidd, Sue Monk Award-winning novelist and former Christian writer whose autobiographical *Dance of the Dissident Daughter* gives an account of her journey from Christianity to goddess worship. Kidd's spirituality incorporates any belief or practice to which her inner instinct responds; her inner voice—the divinity within her—and her connection with nature became her life's sacred authority. Expressing common complaints of the neo-pagan goddess community against male-dominated worship, she explains that the confidence she gained in herself and in nature is due to the empowerment she gained from the Divine Feminine, the worship of which she says can be consistent with Christianity.

King Arthur The first written accounts of King Arthur are attributed to a Welsh monk named Geoffrey Monmouth (d. 1155), who introduced the wizard Merlin and explained how Arthur was born (*History of the Kings of*

Briton). The legend was further developed by Chretien de Troyes in *Le Conte du Graal*, which focuses on the knight Perceval; the "grail" is a flat serving dish. The round table, the sword in the stone, and the chalice from the Last Supper are added to the legend by Robert de Boron's trilogy: *Joseph d'Arimathie, Merlin,* and *Perceval* (*DVC,* 375).

King, Karen L. Author of *The Gospel of Mary of Magdala: Jesus and the First Woman Apostle,* an academic work that adheres to *The Da Vinci Code*'s Mary Magdalene thesis.

King's College Various institutions bear this name, but the one *The Da Vinci Code* refers to is King's College, London (377), the oldest and largest of the University of London's colleges. Established in 1829 by King George IV (an historical fact *DVC* states correctly), King's College was an institution of the Church of England; today it is a large, secular university with a department of theology and religion. Given its age and location, it has a vast breadth and depth of archival materials.

Knights Hospitaller, The Before the Crusades began, a hostel had been established by Benedictine monks in Jerusalem that provided care and shelter for pilgrims. In 1118, a massacre of more than three hundred encouraged the order's master to also provide protection for travelers to the city. These monks wore armor and tunics that bore the symbol of the Christian cross.

Knights of the Rosy Cross, The As a part of Masonic ritual, an "apron of the Rosy Cross" is given the man being initiated as a Rosicrucian knight. This apron, to be worn over the right shoulder and under the left arm, is the "Badge of Knighthood of the Rosy Cross of the Royal Order of Scotland." See also Rosicrucians.

Knights Templar, The Officially the Order of the Poor Knights of Christ and the Temple of Solomon; founded in 1118 by Hugh de Payens, who, along with fellow crusaders, appealed to King Baldwin II of Jerusalem that they might form a religious order—taking the traditional vows of poverty and chastity but with the special purpose of protecting pilgrims traveling to the Holy Land. Baldwin agreed and provided them shelter in the palace, also the former site of Solomon's temple.

The small group of knights grew, due to the efforts of Hugh and fellow knight Andrew of Montbard, as they traveled in search of donations and recruits. One influential supporter was Bernard of Clairvaux, an abbot who had fought in a crusade and was a powerful man within Christendom. Bernard provided a "rule" (book of guidelines) for the Knights and obtained the pope's blessing upon the order. In 1147, the pope added a red cross to the white tunics the Templars wore over their armor, like other military monks, such as the Knights Hospitaller and the Knights of the Holy Sepulchre.

Dan Brown portrays the Knights as having wealth beyond kings, of living beyond the pope's rule, and, most important to *The Da Vinci Code*'s conspiratorial theme, the keepers of a great secret (158–59, 346). The Templars did have wealth, but since they held vows of poverty, their prosperity came from contributions—their money simply accumulated. In fact, the Knights Hospitaller possessed far greater wealth than the Templars.

The Da Vinci Code claims that Pope Clement V devised a plan with France's King Philip IV to arrest, torture, and even kill all the Knights because they were "heretics guilty of devil worship, homosexuality, defiling the cross, sodomy, and other blasphemous behavior" (160). In reality, Philip's envy of Templar wealth and power provoked him, independent of Clement V, to order the arrest of all Templars on October 13, 1307. Clement was notified later; he was appalled but could not annul the trials due to many Templars having been coerced into confessing bizarre crimes while placed under the severe torture of Philip's soldiers. Eventually Clement was persuaded to suppress the Knights, but he was not the formulator or initiator of the plan to extinguish them.

Koyaanisqatsi The title of a 1980s documentary; the first of the trilogy QATSI, produced by Reggio. *Koyaanisqatsi*, says the film, is a Hopi word that means "life out of balance" or "life of moral corruption and turmoil." The documentary contrasts the evils of a technological, urban society with the peace and goodness of the natural environment.

The Da Vinci Code asserts that Christianity brought wars, abuse of women, and disrespect for "Mother Earth"; its male-dominance obliterated the perfection that the pagan dualist "sacred feminine" had produced (125–26—spelled "Koyanisquatsi"). Historically, no such society has ever existed.

L source Scholarly term; shorthand reference to information about Jesus unique to the gospel of Luke. See also M source; Q.

L'isa Dan Brown's fictitious alternative spelling of "Isis." According to *The Da Vinci Code,* the name of Leonardo's *Mona Lisa* is an anagram of "Amon" and "L'isa"—two Egyptian deities said to have represented the principles of male and female fertility. However, "L'isa" is not an alternate spelling of "Isis," and the painting known in the English-speaking world as *Mona Lisa* was never known as such in either its native country or its current country of residence; Italy knows it as *La Gioconda* and France as *La Joconde.* See also Amon; Isis; Leonardo da Vinci; *Mona Lisa.*

Labrys axe Double-headed axe widely used in Neolithic, Minoan, and Greek societies; apparently used in sacrificial rites, which often alluded to a Mother Goddess; also used by mythical Amazon and Scythian female warriors. Modern goddess-cult advocates find the labrys axe to be an alluring symbol; medieval charms were also crafted in the axe's likeness, thought to be useful in attracting women. *The Da Vinci Code*'s Jacques Saunière is a renowned collector of goddess art, including labrys axes from Delphi (23).

Last Supper, The Leonardo mural, painted upon a refectory (dining hall) wall in Santa Maria delle Grazie (church) in Milan, Italy. When commissioned around 1493, Leonardo was the court painter for Ludovico Sforza, governor of Milan; completing it took him four years. Dan Brown calls *The Last Supper* a fresco—a painting applied to a surface while the plaster is still wet. It is more accurately a mural; Leonardo's meticulous style was ill-suited for the quick-drying plaster that is the fresco's defining element.

Leonardo experimented with a mixture of oil and tempera paint that he applied to the wall's dry stone surface. Unfortunately, the technique was not successful, and reports of deterioration came as early as 1517. Many attempts have been made to restore the original colors and details of the image, resulting in a presentation that contains little of the original paint.

The Last Supper is held up by The Da Vinci Code's Leigh Teabing as proof of the unique relationship between Jesus and Mary Magdalene (242–43); supporting evidence, allegedly, can be found in (1) the absence of a traditional grail or communion cup, (2) the questionable identity of the figure seated at Jesus' right hand, and (3) the overall composition and obvious symbology of the painting. Sources provided for this interpretation are several books (DVC, 253), one of which—The Templar Revelation: Secret Guardians of the True Identity of Christ—is an actual publication, a source Brown used for his strange take on Leonardo's art.

The mural's subject matter is the Passover Meal that Jesus shared with his disciples prior to his arrest and crucifixion. Two separate accounts of this event are found in the Christian New Testament. The first is told in the gospels of Mark (14:12–25), Matthew (26:17–29), and Luke (22:7–23); here Jesus raises a cup and says, "This is my blood of the covenant, which is poured out for many" (Mark 14:24). Each gospel says that Jesus held up or referred to "a cup" or "his cup," and there is no reference to a special chalice used by Jesus alone and then passed around the table—nothing suggests that each disciple did not still have his own cup before him as they all participated. The grail image with which contemporary readers are familiar originated in the 1170 poem Perceval, not the New Testament gospels. The lack of a chalice in Leonardo's painting is an indicator of his thoughtfulness rather than a scheme to present an elaborate code for future generations.

The second description of the Passover Meal is found in John's gospel (13:21–30). When Sophie Neveu recalls Jesus' words that have become part of Communion ritual, she's remembering the accounts found in the Synoptics (DVC, 236); no such words are recorded by John, whose account includes Jesus washing the disciples' feet (vv. 4–11) followed by the revelation that one disciple will betray him. It is this description of the Passover Meal that most art historians agree is depicted in Leonardo's famous mural.

The seating in question is fairly clear in John's record. The disciple "whom Jesus loved" was close enough to lean upon Jesus (21:20); "this is the disciple who testifies to these things and who wrote them down. We know that his testimony is true" (v. 24). While Mary Magdalene may have been in the room during the meal, she is not one of the disciples in *The Last Supper*. John's feminine appearance is not unique to this painting or to this figure; men in Renaissance art often appear angelic, fragile, and somewhat androgynous. Leonardo's own notes about the placement of figures in the mural affirm without question that the figure seated next to Jesus is John.

Leigh Teabing also finds mystery in Leonardo's composition, noting that the space between Jesus and John makes the shape of the letter V, which he claims to be a symbol for the female womb. Teabing then highlights the shape of an M formed by the figures of Jesus and the person seated at his right hand; this M, supposedly, must stand for "Mary Magdalene."

Those who carefully view *The Last Supper* will see that Leonardo does indeed use composition to emphasize the upheaval and uncertainty elicited by Jesus' announcement that a disciple would betray him. That Jesus is the central figure is emphasized by the openness around him and the clever use of three open windows for added depth. The disciples are grouped in threes and are turned and twisted in various ways to show their confusion. The "disembodied" hand (*DVC*, 248) Teabing observes actually belongs to Peter and is holding a bread knife. Leonardo's notes explain that one disciple turns his hand and its knife so quickly that it knocks over a glass of wine; most art historians interpret the knife in Peter's hand to be a foreshadowing of the sword he will use a few hours later to defend Jesus in the garden (not of his anger toward Jesus' love for Mary Magdalene [247]). See also Renaissance.

Latin cross Recognizable Christian symbol; depicted with a long vertical beam and a shorter horizontal beam close to (but not even with) the top of the vertical beam. Commonly thought to represent the Roman crucifixion method that Jesus suffered; the Latin cross with the figure of Jesus upon it is called a crucifix (*DVC*, 145). See also crucifix.

left and right *The Da Vinci Code* contends that *left* has been deemed as something "sinister," because the church attempted to defame it.

However, negative connotation predates Christianity; prior to any Christian influence, the Latin word for *left* was *sinister,* and the (positive) word for *right* was *dextera.* Furthermore, the "left brain" is not associated with irrationality but with rationality. Also, the concept of "left" in non-Christian cultures—India is an example, with "left-hand tantra"—is considered negative.

Leonardo da Vinci A true Renaissance man; d. 1519; Leonardo was likely born at Anchiano, Italy, but was reared in Vinci, west of Florence. He was born to an unmarried peasant named Caterina, about whom little is known. He was educated at home by his father, a prominent lawyer, though much of his encyclopedic knowledge apparently came through independent study.

Serving an apprenticeship under noted Florentine artist Andrea del Verrocchio—whose patron, or financial supporter, was Lorenzo de Medici (the Magnificent)—Leonardo early demonstrated formidable talent as a painter, and through Lorenzo he became connected with many influential thinkers and artists. However, maintaining essential economic support (patronage) proved difficult for him; that, combined with the ongoing outbreak of warfare, caused him to move frequently.

In 1482, at age thirty, Leonardo relocated to design military weapons for the duke of Milan. This was not such a great leap for an artist; during the Renaissance, war was viewed as an art form, and, more significantly, Leonardo never studied an area but what he mastered it.

During his late forties, Leonardo was back in Florence after nearly two decades, but he would soon leave once more to become military engineer for the commander of the papal armies. He later returned again to Florence, then made still another move to Milan in 1506.

LEONARDO

1452—born to unmarried peasant girl, Caterina; father was well-known attorney

1469—became an apprentice under Verrocchio and acquainted with Lorenzo de Medici

1476—accused of sodomy; case dropped for lack of evidence

1476—began designing unique war machine

1482—wrote letter emphasizing his military skills; barely referenced that he was a painter; moved from Florence to Milan

1485—began designing giant crossbow; designed helicopter (aerial screw)

1487—began designing flying machines; did first anatomical sketch; military tank, deep-sea-diving suit; drew *Vitruvian Man*

1489—commissioned to cast largest equestrian statue ever built

At age sixty he fled to Rome, but younger artists (like Michelangelo and Raphael) had preceded him there for patronage, so he continued on to France. François I, who became his patron, was the first who seemed to fully grasp his genius. When a stroke rendered painting impossible, Leonardo continued designing until his death on May 2, 1519.

The breadth and quality of his accomplishments have caused Leonardo to be labeled "a genius of all geniuses." Two of his works, *Mona Lisa* and *The Last Supper,* rank among the world's finest and figure prominently in Dan Brown's *The Da Vinci Code* for their allegedly secret symbols. In addition, Louvre curator Jacques Saunière's body is found in the posture of Leonardo's *Vitruvian Man.*

Leonardo's interests were nearly innumerable: music, solar power, mathematics, architecture, anatomy, philosophy, astronomy, aviation, weaponry, et al. His notebooks contain remarkably apt drawings of helicopters, bridges, machine guns, tanks, and submarines. Virtually none of his inventive ideas was implemented, but his mind was clearly one of the most creative in human history. Ironically, his scientific writings were largely unknown until centuries later, and when he moved to France in his later years, this underappreciated artist arrived with *Mona Lisa* in his baggage, certainly unaware of carrying what would become one of the world's most prized paintings.

The Da Vinci Code portrays Leonardo as blatantly anti-Catholic or, more generally, anti-Christian. What he precisely believed is unclear, but he did perceive of science as understanding the God who had created nature. To him, God was the First Mover of all, "the Light of all things" who designed all things.

LEONARDO
(cont.)

1490—adopted a ten-year-old

1495—began painting *The Last Supper* (later underwent numerous restorations)

1499—briefly in Venice

1500—began designing a glider; moved back to France

1502— left Florence to travel Italy with Cesare Borgia, commander of papal armies

1503—began work on *Mona Lisa*

1505—returned to the study of anatomy and of muscles

1506—moved back to Milan

1510—began to study respiratory system

1513—began study of the heart; began painting *St. John the Baptist;* moved to Rome; unlike Michelangelo and Raphael, was unable to find patronage

1517—moved to France, to the Loire Valley; eventually suffered a stroke

1519—died at age 67

While most of his religious views are not well-known, and although he struggled with specific religious patterns, he was by no means an agnostic or atheist (as some have portrayed him). Allegations as to his sexual orientation are equally undemonstrated; contrary to Brown's claims, there is no evidence that he was homosexual. He was once accused of sodomy, but the charges were dropped.

Brown states that Leonardo produced great quantities of Christian art and "hundreds of lucrative Vatican commissions" (*DVC*, 45), but Leonardo often didn't even complete his works; excluding his drawings, he produced fewer than thirty paintings. He started far more projects than he finished—several factors (including wars and failure to secure patronage) likely contributed to this, but the primary cause was most likely his perfectionism. His genius became the enemy of completion when he was concerned he could not work flawlessly. Brown also would have us believe Leonardo was the recipient of numerous commissions for Pope Leo X, when in reality he didn't even spend much time in Rome.

The shadow of Leonardo that permeates *The Da Vinci Code* is essentially cast without the mass of historical substance. See also Brown, Dan; *Last Supper;* Louvre; *Mona Lisa;* Saunière, Jacques; Renaissance; Roman Catholic Church; *Vitruvian Man.*

Les Dossiers Secrets See *Dossiers Secrets, Les.*

Leigh, Richard Coauthor of *Holy Blood, Holy Grail.* See also Baigent, Michael.

Leucius (or Leucius Charinus) Fourth-century Christian writer; Augustine and Epiphanius believed that he wrote at least five of the apocryphal *Acts.* See *Acts of Andrew; Acts of John; Acts of Paul; Acts of Peter; Acts of Thomas;* Augustine of Hippo; Epiphanius of Salamis.

Light of the world (as borrowed from Mithras) Dan Brown contends that Christians borrowed the notion of Jesus as "Light of the world" from Mithraism (*DVC*, 232). There is no evidence that this occurred; more likely, the converse is true. See Christianity as "borrowed"; December 25; Mithras.

Lincoln, Henry Coauthor of *Holy Blood, Holy Grail.* See also Baigent, Michael.

lingua pura, la Italian, "the pure language"; here referring to English. *The Da Vinci Code* presents the very meter of a poetic line as having pagan aspects and secret significance, specifically regarding the iambic pentameter from Leonardo's notebook (303). Inexplicably, to Dan Brown, that alleged secret societies were suppressed by the church is of great import. See iambic pentameter.

Louvre, The One of the world's finest art museums; located in the center of Paris. The first building on the site was a fort built by Philip II in 1190; in 1546 it was largely transformed into a royal chateau; in 1793 French revolutionaries seized all royal properties and made the Louvre a museum. The Louvre houses some of the world's most renowned works of art, including the priceless *Winged Victory, Venus de Milo,* and, of course, *Mona Lisa,* a prominent *Da Vinci Code* feature.

Lunn, Martin Author of *Da Vinci Code Decoded;* states that he is "Grand Master of the Dragon Society." Lunn follows Dan Brown's conspiracy theories about the church having long tried to hide and suppress truth.

Lutzer, Erwin W. Author of *The Da Vinci Code Deception: Credible Answers to the Questions Millions Are Asking About Jesus, the Bible, and The Da Vinci Code.*

LXX Roman numerals for "seventy"; abbreviation for the Septuagint. See Septuagint.

M source Scholarly term; shorthand for information about Jesus unique to Matthew's gospel. See also *Gospel of the Hebrews;* L source; Q.

Maccabees, The Prominent Jewish family, second century BC. Beginning with the revolt of Judas Maccabeus against the Seleucid (Syrian) Antiochus IV (Epiphanes), the family gained independence for the Jewish people that lasted until 63 BC, when the Romans conquered the Holy Land. Stories of the Maccabees can be found in four apocryphal books that appear in Roman Catholic (*1* and *2 Maccabees*) and Eastern Orthodox (*1, 2, 3,* and *4 Maccabees*) Old Testaments. See also apocrypha; Bible; canon.

"Madonna Lisa" Leonardo's biographer, Giorgio Vasari, first attributed this name to Leonardo's portrait of a woman with an intriguing smile. The Italian word *madonna* literally means "madame," and Vasari believed the woman depicted was Madame Lisa Gherardini del Giocondo. Leonardo himself attributed no title to the portrait. See *Mona Lisa.*

Madonna of the Rocks See *Virgin of the Rocks.*

Magdalene Diaries, The In *The Da Vinci Code,* "Magdalene Diaries" refers to a document allegedly written by Mary Magdalene, recording her relationship with Jesus, the events surrounding the Crucifixion, and her experiences in France. Dan Brown's Leigh Teabing claims these documents are part of a larger collection of secret manuscripts known as "Sangreal" (256); in reality, the only known *Magdalene Diaries* is a Robert Grant novel (2005).

Malleus Maleficarum Latin for "Witches' Hammer" (also known as *Hexenhammer*); penned in the fifteenth century, primarily by German monk Heinrich Kramer. According to *The Da Vinci Code*, "The Catholic Inquisition published the book that arguably could be called the most blood-soaked publication in human history. *Malleus Maleficarum*—or *The Witches' Hammer*—indoctrinated the world to 'the dangers of freethinking women' and instructed the clergy how to locate, torture, and destroy them" (125).

In fact, the Catholic Church did *not* publish *Malleus Maleficarum,* and the Inquisition actually *condemned* its views.

While writing, Kramer directed a trial at Innsbruck, where he investigated fifty-seven suspected witches. The bishop of Brixen became so disgusted by Kramer's fascination with the witches' sexual behavior that he stopped the trial, declaring that the devil was not in the witches but in Kramer. *Malleus Maleficarum* clearly reflected his own vulgar sexual preoccupations.

In 1487, Kramer attempted to have the book approved by the Catholic faculty of Cologne University; they rejected it because its legal procedures were unethical and because Kramer's demonology differed radically from the church's understanding of Scripture. In response, Kramer forged a glowing letter of approval and claimed it came from them. The Inquisition condemned Kramer and his book in 1490.

In the sixteenth and seventeenth centuries, *Malleus Maleficarum* did become popular among secular and Protestant judges; until publication of John Bunyan's *Pilgrim's Progress* in 1678, it was Europe's second-most-popular book. Nevertheless, it wasn't used in the Inquisition, but primarily in secular courts. Furthermore, although its recommendations were applied in some cases, there is little evidence that its procedures were followed throughout Europe. Its long-term popularity was likely due to its prurient appeal rather than in its usefulness in locating and trying witches. See also Inquisition; witch-hunts.

manuscript Term used in the field of textual criticism to refer to a complete or near-complete copy of an ancient document. See also autograph; codex; papyrus; textual criticism.

Marcion of Sinope Gnostic leader; d. c. 160; wealthy son of the leading
pastor of Sinope in the region of Pontus, near the Black Sea; reinterpreted
the life of Jesus and attracted a large mid-second-century following. Marcion believed that the Old Testament deity who created the world was
not the Father of Jesus Christ but an evil god; the physical world, as such,
was also evil.

Marcion produced for his followers (the Marcionites) an edition of
the Scriptures edited to fit his theology. The resulting "Bible" included
only Luke's gospel and Paul's letters—nothing more, with all references to
the Old Testament expunged. Although the church in Rome excluded
Marcion from their fellowship, his teachings continued to spread before
fading in the fourth and fifth centuries. See also canon; Gnosticism.

Marquis de Sade (Donatien Alphonse François de Sade) d. 1814; a
notorious libertine whose prolific pornographic writings still elicit interest
among some devotees of sexual liberation. His ideas stemming from his
scandalous obsession with violent sexuality landed him in prison and a
mental hospital. In 1803, he was declared insane and spent his final years
in an asylum. The word *sadistic* comes from his name.

The marquis was an aristocrat who served as a soldier during the
Seven Years War. He married and had three children with his first wife
(and carried on an affair with her sister). His interest in Enlightenment
philosophy was evident in the atheism espoused in *A Dialogue Between a
Priest and a Dying Man* (1782). In novels like *120 Days of Sodom, Justine,*
and *Juliette,* he delved into the darker depths of violent pornography. He
lived profligately, enjoying and abusing prostitutes of both sexes; after dis-
tributing what he thought was an aphrodisiac (actually poisonous), he was
brought to trial and sentenced to death, though the king granted him a
reprieve in 1772.

In his final days he began advocating utopian socialism; in the twentieth century, existentialists and feminists like Simone de Beauvoir (mistress of Jean-Paul Sartre and author of *The Second Sex,* a bible of femi-
nism) defended him as an advocate of sexual liberation. Despite his
"sadism," he enjoys a positive regard in some sectors of the radical left
(*DVC,* 88).

marriage, Jewish According to Dan Brown, Jesus must have been married because first-century Jewish "social decorum . . . [would] virtually forbid a Jewish man to be unmarried" (*DVC*, 245). Although marriage was the norm in Jewish culture, no "social decorum" would have prevented Jesus from remaining single. In fact, Jewish tradition includes a long line of unmarried prophets and devotees. For instance, Elijah and Jeremiah were single, the Essenes forbade marriage, and John the Baptist seems to have remained single throughout his life. See also Essenes; Mary Magdalene.

Mars The "red planet," circling the sun in our galaxy. In Roman mythology, Mars was the god of war, of springtime, and—in some cases—of fertility. He was often regarded as the father of Romulus and Remus, legendary founders of the city of Rome; as such, Romans were known as "sons of Mars." Mars often represents the strong, masculine traits of a warrior; books like John Gray's *Men Are from Mars, Women Are from Venus* indicate the influence of this symbolism (*DVC*, 237).

Mary Magdalene According to the New Testament, Mary Magdalene was a disciple of Jesus from whom he cast "seven demons"; she followed him throughout his ministry, witnessed the crucifixion, and, with two other female disciples, discovered the empty tomb. Mary was probably from Magdala, a village on the western shore of the Sea of Galilee.

   The Da Vinci Code alleges that the New Testament excludes an important fact: "The marriage of Jesus and Mary Magdalene is part of the historical record" (245). There is no evidence in any first-century record that implies a sexual or marital relationship between Jesus and Mary Magdalene. Additionally, even if Jesus had married—again, a proposition for which there is no reliable evidence—it wouldn't be destructive to Christian faith (as Dan Brown implies), for the Scriptures neither affirm nor deny that Jesus was married.

   The Da Vinci Code notes that Mary Magdalene was not a prostitute: "That unfortunate misconception is the legacy of a smear campaign launched by the early church. The church needed to defame Mary Magdalene to cover up her dangerous secret [i.e., Mary's role as the spouse of Jesus]" (244).

   There is no biblical evidence that she was a prostitute. Jesus cast seven demons out of Mary (Luke 8:2), but there is no biblical data to suggest she was sexually immoral. At the same time, there is also no evidence to suggest that anyone instituted a "smear campaign" to discredit her. A tradition arose in the third and fourth centuries that she was the sinful woman mentioned in Luke 7:36–50 and, perhaps, the woman caught in adultery in John 7:53–8:11; in 591, Pope Gregory I included this teaching in a sermon. Although such identifications were probably mistaken, they are far from a slander crusade launched to hide a dangerous secret. See also Benjamin, tribe of; *Gospel of Mary; Gospel of Philip;* marriage, Jewish.

Mary, Mother of Jesus One of four Marys identified in the canonical (New Testament) Gospels; one of five women Matthew's gospel (1:16) lists in the genealogy of Jesus, unusual for a time in which genealogies traced lineage through fathers. The angel Gabriel refers to Mary as "highly favored" (Luke 1:28); she was present when Jesus was crucified (John 19:25), and she was with the disciples (Acts 1:14) after the ascension, following the resurrection. In 451, the Council of Chalcedon declared Mary to be "*theotokos,*" a Greek word meaning "God-bearer." In stark contrast to Dan Brown's imaginary "smear campaign" against women that *The Da Vinci Code's* fictitious church has long promoted, Roman Catholics, Eastern Orthodox, and Protestant Christians recognize Mary as an example of humility, trust, courage, strength, and devotion worthy of the Creator's favor.

Mary, sister of Martha and Lazarus The New Testament Gospels depict this Mary as the one who anoints Jesus and wipes his feet with her hair (John 11–12); she also sat at his feet and listened to his teaching (Luke 10:38–42). Jesus violated cultural norms by welcoming a female to take a position that Jewish society had reserved for men (the role of disciple); Jesus defied society by valuing and honoring women, affirming their immeasurable intrinsic worth.

Masons, The See Freemasonry.

Masoretic Text, The From Hebrew *mesorah,* "passing on a tradition." The Masoretic is the Hebrew text of the Jewish Scriptures, compiled by Jewish scribes in the seventh century.

Melito of Sardis Christian bishop of Sardis in Asia Minor; d. c. 180;

according to Tertullian and Jerome, esteemed for his prophetic powers. Although Melito wrote many treatises mentioned by Origen and Eusebius, very little of his writings survived. He sent a defense of the Christian faith to Emperor Marcus Aurelius, and he listed Old Testament books he considered canonical; he did not include the apocryphal books. Some of his ideas seemed to work their way into Arianism a century later; according to Origen, Melito, in some sense, thought of God as a physical entity. See also apocrypha; Arianism; Arius of Alexandria; canon; Eusebius of Caesarea; Origen of Alexandria.

Merovingian The Germanic Franks began invading the Roman empire as early as the mid-third century, and by the time of Constantine they'd gained considerable power in the areas now known as France and Germany. The Franks granted themselves a royal lineage based on their belief in a powerful ancestor named Merovech; they ruled through the seventh century.

One Merovingian king was a Christian named Clovis (began his rule in 481, when the Western empire fell to barbarians); he is credited for naming Paris as his capital. (*The Da Vinci Code* wrongly claims the Merovingians founded Paris.) According to Dan Brown, Dagobert II was brutally murdered in an attempt to end the Merovingian bloodline; he was the last of the Merovingian kings to wield significant power. One of his descendants was Godefroi de Bouillon, supposed founder of the Priory of Sion (*DVC*, 257–58). See also Dagobert II; Godefroi de Bouillon; Paris; Priory of Sion.

Messiah From Hebrew *Moshiakh*, "anointed one." In Deuteronomy 18:17–19, God had promised to raise up a prophet from among his people. Over time he revealed that this prophet would also be a

MEROVINGIANS TO CAROLINGIANS

481—Clovis I, a Merovingian, became King of the Franks

496—Clovis converted to Christianity

511—Clovis died; kingdom divided among his quarrelsome sons

558—The only remaining son, Chlothar I, united the kingdom

561—Chlothar I died; his sons (Charibert I, Guntram, Sigibert, Chilperic I) then repeated the infighting process

567—Charibert I died

575—Sigibert murdered

584—Chilperic murdered

584-629—Chlothar II reigned (son of Chilperic I)

592—Guntram died

639—Dagobert I died

king, a descendant of David whose kingdom would last forever (Ps. 89:27–29). Because anointing accompanied a king's selection (1 Sam. 10:1; 16:13), this promised prophet, the "anointed one," became known as *Messiah*. See also Christology.

metaphor The word has Greek roots, meaning "to transfer"; a figure of speech comparing unrelated items to provide clarity or imaginative insight. Shakespeare's famous line "All the world's a stage / And all the men and women merely players" is a metaphor. Unlike similes, metaphors rarely use the words *like* or *as*. (For instance, "this is like that," or "A is to B as B is to C.")

Metzger, Bruce Professor at Princeton Theological Seminary; defender of the New Testament textual tradition's authenticity. Significant writings include: *The Canon of the New Testament;* "Literary Forgeries and Canonical Pseudepigrapha" (*Journal of Biblical Literature* 91 [1972]); *The Text of the New Testament: Its Transmission, Corruption, and Restoration* (3rd ed., with Michael D. Coogan); and *The Oxford Companion to the Bible.*

Miesel, Sandra, and Carl E. Olson Authors of *The Da Vinci Code Hoax.*

MEROVINGIANS TO CAROLINGIANS (cont.)

679—Dagobert II killed

687—Pépin d'Héristal began to reunite Frankish territories

714—Pépin's son Charles Martel began to expand the kingdom

732—Charles Martel repelled the Muslim advance (Battle of Tours); Carolingian comes from his name

751—The pope anointed Martel's son Pépin II (the Short) a "divinely sanctioned king," fusing the Frankish monarchy into the papal order

768—Pépin II's son (Pépin d'Héristal's great-grandson) Charlemagne ascended to the throne

800—Charlemagne crowned emperor by the pope in Rome

---

minstrel, minister Dan Brown asserts that "minister" and "minstrel" come from the same root word, presumably the Latin *ministra,* meaning "servant" or "attendant" (*DVC,* 390). However, the usage of "minister" as a description of a priest or pastor more likely derives from the Latin *magister*—someone duly authorized to conduct specific services.

Whether or not *ministra* is the root for Christian usage of "minister," *minstrel* didn't function as a description for traveling musicians until the late thirteenth century (long after "minister" became a descriptive term for church leaders); prior to this, professional poets employed by a king were more commonly known as *scops,* while traveling performers were known as *gleemen.* Brown's attempt to connect Christian usage of "minister" with medieval "minstrels" reveals either shoddy scholarship or an effort to deceive.

Mishnah Hebrew for "repetition"; traditions passed down from the Jewish rabbis, gathered by Rabbi Judah Ha-Nasi around AD 200. Commentaries on the *Mishnah* are known as *Gemara* (Hebrew for "completion"). Together, the *Mishnah* and the *Gemara* form the *Talmud* (Aramaic for "teaching"). See also *Talmud.*

Mithras Persian sun god whose worship pervaded the Roman empire during its Christian era; syncretistic mystery religion, especially favored by soldiers and rulers; featured the ritual killing of bulls. Dan Brown makes much of similarities between Mithraism and Christianity, asserting that nothing was "new" in the latter (*DVC,* 232); much of this thinking was advanced in *The Christ Conspiracy* by Acharya S.

According to *The Da Vinci Code* and to *The Christ Conspiracy,* Mithras was born on December 25, was called "Son of God and Light of the World," and rose from the grave. The theories of Acharya S are easy to refute; furthermore, because adherents to Mithraism (like Freemasons) were committed to absolute secrecy, few documents survived, and little is known about them.

When Christianity "borrows" terms, it generally gives the word (or concept) new content. Even so, there is no evidence of this occurring with regard to Mithras worship—more likely, Mithraism borrowed from Christianity, as early Christians were exclusivists, whereas Mithraism was syncretistic (borrowed from multiple religions). See Christianity as "borrowed."

modernity Historical era, extending roughly from the eighteenth century to the twentieth century. Prior to the sixteenth-century Reformation, the traditions of the Roman Catholic Church provided the intellectual framework by which Europeans interpreted their faith and their experiences. After the Reformation, especially in Protestant regions, a new interpretative framework emerged—*human reason*—that provided the intellectual basis for the epoch now known as "modernity" or "the Modern Age."

A philosophical movement known as the Enlightenment marked its beginning; applied to science, modernity resulted in Isaac Newton's understanding of the universe as a vast machine with specific and unbreakable laws. Applied to religion, modernity resulted first in Deism, a widespread belief in a rational deity who created the universe with certain natural laws, but no longer involves himself with his creation. Later, modernity led to a division among those who considered themselves Christians: some applied human reason to the Scriptures and treated anything that seemed not to fit natural laws—including miracles—as the mistaken impressions of primitive people; this practice marked the beginnings of theological liberalism. Others, like Charles Hodge and B. B. Warfield, attempted to defend the Bible with human reason; these individuals became known as fundamentalists and, later, as evangelicals.

Especially in Europe, the Modern Age was marked by intense optimism, a belief that humanity was continually improving—the concept of inevitable upward human progress. As such, it isn't surprising that Charles Darwin's evolutionary hypotheses became popular. A century of relatively increasing peace seemed to confirm this worldview.

The death of modernity began in the early twentieth century. During the First World War, the technology that people had seen as indications of increasing wisdom and intelligence became tools to destroy humanity. See also postmodernity; Reformation. (For in-depth discussions of modernity and postmodernity, see Thomas Oden, *Requiem,* and Stanley Grenz, *A Primer on Postmodernism.*)

Mona Lisa Leonardo's renowned portrait, made with oil on poplar; painted around 1503. There is speculation as to who commissioned the work, but it's clear the patron did not receive the finished painting, because Leonardo took it, along with a portrait of John the Baptist, when he moved to France in 1516. King Francis I bought the portrait, and during the next several centuries it was housed in various sites, eventually coming to the Louvre.

We do not have any of Leonardo's notes about the woman

portrayed—not even her name. In 1550, almost thirty years after his death, Giorgio Vasari wrote a biography of Leonardo in which he refers to this piece as *Mona Lisa,* or *Madonna Lisa,* which simply means "Madame Lisa." *Mona* means "Lady," so the picture is of "Lady Lisa." Vasari explains that the woman was Lisa Gherardini del Giocondo, wife of Francesco del Giocondo, a silk merchant, which is why many Italians call the painting "La Gioconda."

The picture was not particularly praised or prized until the nineteenth century. Then, as Romantics reveled in the "feminine mystique," *Mona Lisa* came to represent everything marvelous and mysterious about women. To Walter Pater, for example, she represented the eternal feminine that is "older than the rocks among which she sits."

We cannot be certain that Vasari's account is accurate; at any rate, the lecture given by *The Da Vinci Code*'s Robert Langdon to a group of prison inmates (119–21) is filled with conclusions without basis in reality. Leonardo gave no explanation as to why he brought *Mona Lisa* to France, but he did not take it with him everywhere he went (119). Nor is there any consensus within the art world concerning one of the "world's most documented insider jokes" (119): no reputable art historian claims to know why she has the sly smile, but there is similarity between her smile and the smile on the face of Leonardo's portrait of John the Baptist, which clearly depicts a man.

The Da Vinci Code says that Leonardo's supposedly well-documented homosexuality contributed to his enlightened perspectives on the need for balance between male and female characteristics. The secret of the *Mona Lisa,* it claims, is that it portrays the fusion of the male and female—that the painted figure is androgynous. There was one incident during Leonardo's youth in which he and three other men were accused of committing sexual crimes with a male prostitute, but the charges were dropped for lack of evidence, and most of Leonardo's personal life remains unknown because he guarded information about it. It's irresponsible to assert that Leonardo intended to send secret anthropological or theological messages through a painting, especially through a title he didn't even give to it. See androgyny; Leonardo da Vinci.

Mother Earth The term has vastly different meanings to different people. To Francis of Assisi, it was the recognition that God had made a good earth that, like a mother, sustains us. To Native Americans, it often meant a divine being; Shawnee warrior Tecumseh said, "The earth is my mother—and on her bosom I will repose." To "deep ecologists" and some Green Party members, it means Gaia, a living, breathing, personal being, ultimately all that is. To pantheistic philosophers, Mother Earth means God. To New Age followers, she is the source of health and wholeness— thus the Wiccan ceremonies and chants designed to bring followers into right relations with her. *The Da Vinci Code* displays a pronounced religious reverence for Mother Earth along with its emphasis upon the "sacred feminine."

Muratorian Fragment, The Late-second-century document; discovered in the 1700s by a priest named Muratori; an ancient listing of books recognized as part of the New Testament canon; called a "fragment" because its first portion is missing. In *The Da Vinci Code,* Dan Brown claims that men who possessed "a political agenda . . . to solidify their own power base" (231–34) established the New Testament canon in the fourth century. The Muratorian Fragment demonstrates that most New Testament books were established in the canon no later than the second century. Accepted by its author were the four gospels, Acts, Paul's letters, Jude, two letters of John (the second of these may include the two books known today as 2 and 3 John), Revelation, and *Wisdom of Solomon.*

Although he personally accepts *Apocalypse of Peter,* the author admits that "some will not allow it to be read in the church." He rejects *Shepherd of Hermas,* stating that "it cannot be read publicly to the people in church either among the Prophets, whose number is complete, or among the Apostles, for it is after their time." Hebrews, James, and 1 and 2 Peter were not yet listed, but the Muratorian Fragment demonstrates that most of the New Testament canon was fixed as early as 170. See also apocrypha; Bible; canon.

myth From a Greek term meaning "narrative"; generally means one of two things: (1) a story telling a great truth (e.g., a "creation myth") enshrouded in poetic language, or (2) a groundless fantasy—as in the "Pocahontas myth" inaccurately portraying Powhatan's daughter during the founding of Jamestown. Writers like J. R. R. Tolkien and C. S. Lewis thought highly of classic myths, and Tolkien, of course, crafted one of his own in *The Lord of the Rings*. One biographer, Humphrey Carpenter, said that Tolkien "believed in the *truth* of mythology. 'Just as speech is invention about objects and ideas,' he said to Lewis . . . 'so myth is invention about truth. We have come from God, and inevitably the myths woven by us, though they contain error, will also reflect a splintered fragment of the true light, the eternal truth that is with God. Indeed only by myth-making, only by becoming a "sub-creator" and inventing stories, can Man ascribe to the state of perfection that he knew before the fall'" (Walter Hooper, quoting from Humphrey Carpenter's *J. R. R. Tolkien*, in preface to *The Collected Works of C. S. Lewis*, 130). When writers like Dan Brown refer to the "myths" of Christianity, however, they generally mean untrue fantasies foisted upon gullible people.

Nag Hammadi Library, The Book (in English) of the Gnostic writings found at Nag Hammadi; as the subtitle states, "The Definitive Translation of the Gnostic Scriptures Complete in One Volume." James M. Robinson, Professor at Claremont Graduate University and founder of the Institute for Antiquity and Early Christianity, is general editor. The single volume contains all fifty-two Gnostic texts from the discovery.

Nag Hammadi papyri, The Collection of more than forty Gnostic documents, unearthed in the mid–1940s near Nag Hammadi in Upper Egypt. According to *The Da Vinci Code,* these are "the earliest Christian records. Troublingly, they do not match up with the gospels in the Bible" (245–46).

The Nag Hammadi documents do not "match up with the gospels in the Bible"—that much is true. The documents found at Nag Hammadi are *not,* however, "the earliest Christian records." The documents in the New Testament were written between AD 40 and 100. Most of the texts at Nag Hammadi were copied between the third and fifth centuries AD. In fact, the *oldest* document at Nag Hammadi is probably *Gospel of Thomas,* which seems to have been written around AD 140—nearly a half-century later than the *latest* New Testament text!

Because so much of Dan Brown's argument in *The Da Vinci Code* hinges on the dates and contents of these texts, we've included a complete listing of the Nag Hammadi documents, with a summary of the contents and the approximate date of each document's original composition.

Document	Approximate Date of Composition	Summary of Contents
Acts of Peter and the Twelve	AD 150–250	Tale of a pearl merchant who turns out to be Jesus; not to be confused with the Christian writing *Acts of Peter* from the late second century
Allogenes	AD 300–350	Refers to Gnostics as members of the race of Seth (*allogenes* means "from another race")
Apocalypse of Adam	AD 160–300	Adam tells Seth how he and Eve became more powerful than their Creator, never explicitly mentions any Christian themes or characters
Apocalypse of James 1	AD 200–300	Supposed dialogue between Jesus and James the brother of Jesus
Apocalypse of James 2	AD 150–180	Supposed dialogue between Jesus and James the brother of Jesus, ending with James' martyrdom
Apocryphon of James	AD 140–160	Mildly Gnostic letter, claiming to come from James the brother of Jesus
Apocryphon of John	AD 160–200	Presents the deity of the Old Testament and creator of the physical world as an evil demi-god

Document	Approximate Date of Composition	Summary of Contents
Asclepius	Uncertain	Greek philosophical tractate
Authoritative Teaching	AD 150–200	Gnostic tractate, urging people to avoid physical pleasures
Book of Thomas the Contender	AD 150–225	Supposed "secret words" spoken by Jesus to Thomas and recorded by Matthias; perhaps connected to the *Gospel of Matthias*
Concept of Our Great Power	AD 300–390	Gnostic description of salvation and of the end of the world
Coptic Apocalypse of Paul	AD 160–260, perhaps later	Describes Paul's supposed ascension through several levels of heaven
Coptic Apocalypse of Peter	AD 250–300	Describes Jesus as if he possessed no physical body
Coptic Gospel of the Egyptians	AD 200–300	Presents Jesus as the reincarnation of Seth, third son of Adam and Eve
Dialogue of the Savior	AD 150–200	Found only in fragments, which present a consistently negative view of sexuality and of women
Discourse on the Eighth and Ninth	AD 150–200	Guide for Gnostics to experience the mystical realm
Epistle of Peter to Philip	AD 180–220	Supposed letter, followed by a Gnostic discourse concerning the nature of Jesus Christ

Document	Approximate Date of Composition	Summary of Contents
Eugnostos the Blessed	Uncertain	Presentation of Gnostic cosmology; some elements may be pre-Christian
Exegesis on the Soul	AD 200–250	Short story, recounting the Gnostic myth of the soul's fall from heaven
Gospel of Philip	AD 160–300	Collection of Gnostic sayings from several previous writings, apparently reflecting the teachings of Valentinus
Gospel of Thomas	AD 130–150	List of supposed sayings of Jesus
Gospel of Truth	AD 250–350	Gnostic reworking of the Creation and of the ministry of Jesus
Hypostatis of the Archons	AD 250–350	Mythological presentation of Gnostic cosmology
Hypsiphrone	Uncertain	Fragments of text describe the descent of a heavenly figure similar to *Sophia*
Interpretation of Knowledge	AD 160–200	Valentinian reinterpretation of the teachings of Jesus and Paul
Marsanes	AD 200–300	Descriptions of Gnostic experience and rituals
Melchizedek	AD 200–300	Fragments of text seem to provide a Gnostic reinterpretation of the Old Testament account of Melchizedek
Origin of the World	AD 290–330	Presentation of Gnostic theology

Document	Approximate Date of Composition	Summary of Contents
Paraphrase of Shem	Uncertain	Fragments, presenting a negative view of sexuality
Prayer of Thanksgiving	AD 150–250	Brief prayer of gratitude for having received *gnosis*
Prayer of the Apostle Paul	AD 160–300	Brief prayer with similarities to *Three Steles of Seth* and *Gospel of Philip*
Republic (Plato)	Uncertain	Gnostic adaptation of the philosopher Plato's classic work
Sentences of Sextus	Uncertain	List of wise sayings
Sophia of Jesus Christ	Uncertain, some portions may stem from the late first or early second centuries	List of supposed questions from the apostles, to which Jesus provides Gnostic answers; probably an adaptation of *Eugnostos*
Teachings of Silvanus	AD 160–220	Unlike other Nag Hammadi documents, not a Gnostic text; emphasizes spiritual growth through self-denial
Testimony of Truth	AD 180–220	Polemic against competing Gnostic groups
Thought of Norea	AD 180–240	Depicts a feminine savior, apparently the counterpart of the biblical figure Seth
Three Steles of Seth	AD 220–260	Includes many Gnostic hymns and prayers

Document	Approximate Date of Composition	Summary of Contents
Thunder, Perfect Mind	Uncertain	A divine female figure, "Thunder," sings hymns about herself; not clearly Gnostic, Jewish, or Christian in origin
Treatise of the Great Seth	Uncertain	Supposedly the words of Jesus to a group of Gnostic believers; Simon of Cyrene is crucified instead of Jesus
Treatise on the Resurrection	AD 180–200	Brief letter denying the future physical resurrection of believers
Trimorphic Protennoia	AD 160–200	Description of the descent of "the First Thought" of God into the world
Tripartite Tractate	AD 200–250	Gnostic description of salvation history and cosmology
Valentinian Exposition on Baptism, Anointing, and the Eucharist	AD 150–180	Gnostic reinterpretations of Chrisian rituals
Zostrianos	AD 260–300	Description of Gnostic cosmology

See also *Apocryphon of John;* Bible; canon; *Coptic Apocalypse of Paul; Coptic Apocalypse of Peter; Coptic Gospel of the Egyptians; Dialogue of the Savior;* Gnosticism; *Gospel of Philip; Gospel of Thomas; Gospel of Truth;* Gospels, canonical.

Newman, Sharan Author of *The Real History Behind The Da Vinci Code.*

New Testament Collection of sacred writings, written and collected between AD 40 and 100; twenty-seven documents accepted by Christians as the authoritative guide for Christian faith and practice. See also Bible; canon; Old Testament.

Newton, Sir Isaac A brilliant and complex man; a Fellow of Trinity College, held the honorary position of Lucasian Professor of Mathematics; extremely anti-Catholic, a self-proclaimed Arian. Newton's writings are considered to be the basis for modern physics, and he associated with such influential figures as John Locke, Gottfried Wilhelm Leibniz, and Sir Robert Boyle. Modern depictions of Newton show an apple dropping on his head, causing him to consider the idea of gravity. Despite his scientific mind, he was also a student of alchemy—he sought the formula that would turn lead into gold. *The Da Vinci Code* lists Newton (1, see also 398) as one of the Grand Masters of the Priory of Sion; however, Newton died (1727) more than two centuries before the Priory of Sion was founded. See Plantard, Pierre; Priory of Sion.

nirvana From Sanskrit: "extinction," "cessation," "extinguishing" (*DVC*, 309); originally a Hindi term meaning the extinction of the flame of life and union with Brahma. Buddhists considered nirvana the death of passion and desire, and the end of the delusions that plague us on earth. Contrary to *The Da Vinci Code,* which suggests nirvana is akin to sexual ecstasy, the state of nirvana is the cessation of all sensations.

Noah *The Da Vinci Code*'s zealous, sinister Silas is an albino, and as such he is identified with the patriarch Noah, who, in the apocryphal *1 Enoch* (105:1–4), is said to have had white skin, like an angel. Albinos have frequently embraced this; in the U.S., their organization is the National Organization for Albinism and Hypopigmentation (NOAH). Some characteristics ascribed to albinos by *The Da Vinci Code*—e.g., having red eyes—are not necessarily true.

Nodier, Charles One of Pierre Plantard's imagined Grand Masters of the fabricated Priory of Sion. What is factual: Nodier, born in 1780 in France, was fascinated with mysticism and formed a secret society using Freemason symbols; he also showed interest in Rosicrucian thought and Theosophy. Although his name is largely unknown today, he did mentor the better known Victor Hugo, which may account for Plantard's placing him, on an invented list of Grand Masters, immediately prior to Hugo. See Freemasonry; Hugo, Victor; Plantard, Pierre; Priory of Sion; Rosicrucians.

Notre Dame-de-la-Mer The oratory at Les Saintes-Maries-de-le-Mer was rebuilt in the ninth century; in the eleventh century the monks of Montmajor created a priory there; in the twelfth century they rebuilt the entire church in order to incorporate the town's structure into the expanding complex. The church is named Notre Dame-de-la-Mer; the bones of Mary Jacobe, Mary Salome, and their servant, Sarah, are said to be buried here. A cult grew surrounding these three saints, and Sarah was depicted with dark skin.

France's Les Saintes-Maries-de-le-Mer is said to be the birthplace of the Black Madonna. May 24–25 are the annual feast days for the cult of the Black Virgin; pilgrims still travel to this site in honor of St. Sarah. *The Da Vinci Code* confuses the legend about this servant girl with the unusual story about Mary Magdalene having a child named Sarah (255). See also Black Madonna; Saintes-Maries-de-le-Mer, Les.

obelisk Slender, four-sided column with a pyra-
mid-shaped top; origins can be traced to the
ancient Assyrian and Egyptian societies; still used
for monuments and memorials. The Washington
Monument in Washington, D.C., is the world's
tallest obelisk. In *The Da Vinci Code*, Silas finds
an obelisk in the Church of Saint-Sulpice (105).

ODAN Acronym for the Opus Dei Awareness
Network, an organization founded in 1991 by a former member of Opus
Dei (*DVC*, 30). The group's purpose is to bring information and counsel-
ing to those concerned for friends or family members who are active
members of Opus Dei. See also Opus Dei.

Odes Apocryphal book of poetry; found in the Eastern Orthodox Old Testament. Includes *Prayer of Manasseh*. See also apocrypha; Bible; canon.

Old Testament Collection of sacred writings, written and collected between
1500 and 400 BC, accepted by Jews and Christians as God's written self-
revelation. Thirty-nine books appear in the Jewish and Protestant Old
Testament; seven additional books appear in the Roman Catholic Old
Testament, and ten in the Eastern Orthodox Old Testament. The additional writings are known as "apocryphal" or "deuterocanonical." See also
apocrypha; Bible; canon; deuterocanonical; New Testament.

Olympic rings According to Dan Brown, the five Olympic rings were a
last-minute substitute for the games' originally intended symbol: the five-
pointed star tied to the goddess Venus (*DVC*, 36–37). Actually the
ancient contests were held in honor of Zeus, not Venus. Also, the

Olympic rings were not a Greek creation; they were designed in 1913 by Frenchman Baron Pierre de Coubertin to represent the five participating continents of Africa, America, Asia, Europe, and "Oceania."

Original copies of *The Da Vinci Code* stated that the ancient Olympic Games were held every four years because the planet Venus traced "a perfect pentacle across the ecliptic sky every four years." That cycle was every eight years, not four, and in later printings of the *DVC*, the "four years" was changed to "eight years" (*DVC*, 36), with the games following the *half-cycles* of Venus. See also pentacle.

operative masons Guilds whose members actually had knowledge and skills to work with stone, in contrast to the speculative masons, practitioners of Freemasonry. See Freemasonry; guilds.

Opus Dei Catholic organization founded by Josemaria Escrivá de Balaguer in 1928; currently eighty thousand members worldwide (laypersons and priests). Escrivá's book *The Way* made controversial statements about the value and necessity of pain; such aspects of belief, along with the organization's great wealth, has made it a target for attacks by those who mistrust the Christian faith in general and the Roman Catholic Church in particular. Dan Brown inaccurately depicts Opus Dei as a monastic order (*DVC*, 28); it does not have monks, and its membership is lay-oriented. See Escrivá de Balaguer, Josemaria.

Order of the Rose-Croix of the Temple of the Grail, The Esoteric French group founded in 1891 by Joséphin Péladan. Much of the false history created by Pierre Plantard about the Priory of Sion was plagiarized from the documents of this order, which had actual ties to the French village Rennes-le-Château and Bérenger Saunière. See Saunière, Bérenger; Plantard, Pierre; Priory of Sion; Rennes-le-Château.

Order de Notre Dame de Sion In 1099, when Godefroi de Bouillon captured Jerusalem, an abbey was built south of the city on a mount called "the hill of sion." (The book *Holy Blood, Holy Grail* proposes that this abbey was where the Cistercian and Templar orders were founded.) The church then took its name from this location, and a group of knights associated with the abbey called themselves the *Chevaliers de l'Order de*

Notre Dame de Sion. Only a few documents contain information about them, and some have mistakenly thought them to refer to an "original" Priory of Sion. There is no evidence that the Priory existed before the 1950s. See Godefroi de Bouillon.

Origen of Alexandria Distinguished early church scholar, born in Alexandria, Egypt; d. c. 250; wrote approximately six thousand works. Raised and educated by Christian parents, Origen was named head of the Catechetical School in Alexandria following Clement's retreat from persecutions there. Origen studied Christian writings as well as the Greek philosophers, and he was eventually ordained as a priest by bishops in Caesarea; the method of ordination was not approved by Demetrius, Bishop of Alexandria, who banished him from the priesthood, but Origen, continuing to write and preach, nevertheless established a school in Caesarea (231) before the persecutions of Emperor Decius, during which he was imprisoned and suffered prolonged torture; this is believed to have caused his death.

Origen's writings were widely read by early church theologians and scholars; unfortunately only a few originals of his writings are known to exist, and much of his teaching was preserved by not-always-reliable translations. *De Principiis,* considered one of his most significant, provides theological commentary on topics including angels, the material world, free will, and Scripture, which he believed has literal, moral, and allegorical meaning. He preferred allegorical interpretation because he believed that everything possesses both material and spiritual qualities.

Students of Origen's Alexandrian school played an important role in the fourth-century battle against Arianism. Near the end of his life, Origen seems to have embraced universalism—the belief that all beings, even Satan, will eventually experience salvation. Furthermore, when beliefs held by some of his extremist followers, the Origenists, caused controversy in the church, the Second Council of Constantinople (553) condemned his teachings. For these reasons, although some Eastern Orthodox Christians recognize Origen as a church father, the Roman Catholic Church does not. See also church fathers.

orthodoxy From Greek *orthodoxa,* "correct opinion"; term used by Irenaeus (second century) to describe the beliefs that Jesus originated and the apostles proclaimed. In Christian theology, "orthodoxy" describes the acceptance of certain essential beliefs about the person and work of Jesus Christ. When capitalized, "Orthodoxy" may refer to churches—such as the Eastern Orthodox and Russian Orthodox—whose origins trace to the eastern half of the ancient Roman empire. See apostle; heresy; Irenaeus of Lyons.

Oxbrow, Mark, and Ian Robertson Coauthors of *Rosslyn and the Grail.*

Oxyrhynchus 840 See *Gospel, Oxyrhynchus 840*

pagan *The Da Vinci Code* says the term *pagan* mostly has negative, satanic connotations because of the Christian church's efforts to eliminate all threats to its own domination. The book also claims the root word for "pagan" is *paganus* and that originally it referred to an uneducated, unbaptized country dweller (36). The novel is misleading in both cases.

Although the Latin *paganus* does refer to "a person who lives in the country," the first usage of "pagan" is found in Christian writings from the fourth century, without any implications of being "satanic"; it simply meant one who was not a baptized follower of Jesus Christ.

paganism Most basically, paganism is the worship of nature as self-generating and divine; one consistent characteristic is focus on *reverence for the creation* in contrast to *worship of God* (cf. Rom. 1:25). Theistic religions, such as Judaism and Christianity, view God as simultaneously transcendent (above and beyond the created order) and immanent (present and available to his creation). Christianity views God as the Divine Creator, and everything else as his creation; paganism predominantly sees "god" as being *within*—within humanity and within creation itself.

Early in *The Da Vinci Code* (7), Robert Langdon has just delivered a lecture about hidden pagan symbols in the stonework of Chartres Cathedral (about fifty miles outside of Paris). Construction began in 1194, but wasn't completed until 1220, and the cathedral was finally dedicated in 1260. It's one of France's grandest examples of Gothic architecture—characterized by magnificent ornamentation, imposing figures, memorials to royalty and saints, and local legends.

Since many symbols have wide appeal and broad meanings, symbols on such an ornate structure could be reinterpreted by a creative imagination to have pagan connections. However, the novel doesn't say what these pagan symbols are, leaving the assertion undemonstrated and unproven.

Pagels, Elaine Distinguished author of *The Gnostic Gospels* and *Beyond Belief: The Secret Gospel of Thomas;* Professor of History at Princeton. In 1965, Dr. Pagels began her graduate studies in Christian history at Harvard, around the same time Professor George MacRae began to receive some of the very first Nag Hammadi-text photocopies seen on U.S. soil. Pagels became part of an elite scholarship group laboring to translate the Coptic writings, and she was on the team that translated the first edition of documents into English, published in 1977. Captivated with Gnostic teachings (of which she has been a leading publicist), she wrote her dissertation about Gnosticism and its conflicts with traditional Christianity.

In 1979, Pagels gained acclaim and attention for *The Gnostic Gospels,* in which she suggests that early Christianity was much different from and more diverse than what is presented in the New Testament. Her feminist ideas and acceptance of alternative scriptures eventually prompted her to leave the Episcopal Church, and she has sought to "rehabilitate" Gnostic ideas as a valid expression of early Christianity. Readers familiar with her studies will recognize her influence upon Dan Brown's novel. (Other writings include *The Johannine Gospel in Gnostic Exegesis* [1973]; *Adam, Eve, and the Serpent* [1989]; *The Gnostic Paul* [1992]; *The Origin of Satan* [1995].)

paleography From Greek, "ancient writing"; the study of ancient forms of writing.

Papias of Hierapolis Apostolic father; d. c. 135; acquainted personally with the first generation of believers after the apostles; provided invaluable testimony about early church beliefs. Papias makes it clear that Christians viewed Jesus as "the Lord" from the beginning and that the canonical gospel of Mark was based on Simon Peter's eyewitness testimony. Papias testified,

> I did not take pleasure . . . in those who speak much, but in those who teach what is true. Nor did I take pleasure in those who relate exotic precepts, but in those who relate the precepts which were given to the faith by the Lord, which came down from the Truth himself.

Also, if any follower of the presbyters [his term for the apostles] happened to come along, I inquired about the sayings of the presbyters, what Andrew said, or what Peter said, or what Philip or what Thomas or James or what John or Matthew or any other of the Lord's disciples. . . .

Mark became Peter's translator; he wrote down accurately whatever he remembered. It was not, however, in exact order, for he neither heard the Lord nor accompanied him. Afterwards, he accompanied Peter. Peter tailored his teachings to the needs of each audience, with no intention of giving a chronological narrative of the Lord's sayings. So, Mark made no mistakes when he wrote these things as he remembered them. Of this, however, Mark took the greatest care—not to leave out anything that he had heard and not to put in any fictitious statement.

The writings of Papias are found in fragmented form in the works of Irenaeus and Eusebius. See also apostolic fathers; Eusebius of Caesarea; Gospels, canonical; Irenaeus of Lyons.

papyrus Writing material used commonly in ancient Egypt; derived from the stalk of the papyrus plant. Strips are laid beside one another, then pressed, dried, and smoothed into a flexible sheet suitable for writing upon. The papyrus could then be rolled into a scroll or folded and cut in order to make a codex (*DVC*, 201). See also codex.

Paris Our focus here is not on the spectacular sights of the world's most famous city, but rather on identifying some of Dan Brown's descriptives. *The Da Vinci Code*'s exhilarating and exhausting twenty-some hours of action takes place in Paris, London, and Edinburgh; however, the novel isn't trustworthy as a map  any more than on history, theology, Scripture, art, architecture, or the life of Leonardo. See also map of Paris, page 202.

- Robert Langdon goes south past the Opera House to Place Vendôme. In reality, to accomplish this, one would have to go north.
- Langdon recalls the original meridian running north from Sacré Coeur to the River Seine, continuing to the Paris observatory. To accomplish

this, reverse the direction, going south from Sacré Coeur instead of north.

- To go from the Tuileries to the Louvre, don't go west (as Brown directs) but rather east.
- Also, Paris was not (as Brown contends) founded by the Merovingians, but by the Parisi, a Gallic tribe. Called Lutetia, it later was captured by Julius Caesar. The Merovingians did not rule Paris—and France—until the sixth century.

parousia Greek, "presence" or "arrival." Reference to the second coming of Jesus Christ.

Pastoral Epistles, The New Testament studies term; 1 and 2 Timothy and Titus, so known because the apostle Paul wrote them to give guidance to pastors. Some scholars have questioned Paul's authorship, but this has been thoroughly refuted by scholars like Gordon Fee (*God's Empowering Presence* [1994]), Thomas Oden (*First and Second Timothy and Titus* [1989]), and G. W. Knight (*The Pastoral Epistles* [1992]). See also Pauline corpus.

Patristic writings From Greek *patres,* "fathers"; referring to the writings of the church fathers. See also church fathers.

Paul Apostle specifically chosen by Jesus Christ. Dan Brown's primary *Da Vinci Code* thesis regarding the New Testament hinges on a particular chronology, one in which Constantine allegedly hijacked the "original" books in AD 325 and substituted (in their place) Matthew, Mark, Luke, and John. Brown's position is indefensible; conservative and liberal scholars agree that Paul wrote about the essence of the gospel (1 Cor. 15:1–4) in the AD 50s, and he attributes what he knew about Jesus to the earliest followers, the original disciples. Paul, a contemporary of Jesus, makes no mention of the writings that Dan Brown claims formed the "original" New Testament. The reason? No such "switch" occurred. (See Peter Jones, "Paul, the Last Apostle" in *The Tyndale Bulletin* [36: 1984].)

Pauline corpus, The New Testament studies term; the writings of the apostle Paul. See also Bible; canon; Pastoral Epistles.

Pei, I. M. (Ieoh Ming) Renowned twentieth-century Chinese architect
who studied at MIT and lived thereafter in the U.S. His award-winning
projects range from the east wing of the National Gallery of Art in Washington, D.C., to *Louvre Pyramide* in Paris to the Bank of China in Hong
Kong.

pentacle (five-pointed star) Ancient symbol found carved on the walls of
Babylonian caves. Early astrologers probably tracked the movements of
the planet Venus and discovered that every eight years its path creates a
perfect five-pointed shape around the sun (*DVC*, 35).

The pentacle as a symbol can be found in many cultures, representing
a myriad of perspectives. Until the twentieth century, it was almost exclu-
sively a symbol of protection (or related positive characteristics). In the
fourteenth-century poem *Sir Gawain and the Green Knight,* the five-
pointed star, the symbol on Sir Gawain's shield, represents the qualities of
knighthood: generosity, courtesy, chastity, chivalry, and piety. For modern
Wicca, the pentacle is also an important ritual symbol, the five points
representing "the five elements": earth, air, water, fire, and spirit.

It's unclear when the pentacle became a symbol for the demonic.
Some claim the teachings of the French occultist Eliphas Levi (d. 1875)
first promoted the inverted pentacle as an occult symbol; Anton LaVey (d.
1997) made it notorious when he founded the Church of Satan in 1966.

In *The Da Vinci Code,* Sophie Neveu tells Robert Langdon that when
she played the Tarot cards, the suit of pentacles was her "indicator";
Langdon makes the connection that the pentacles in the deck of twenty-
two cards mean "femininity" (*DVC*, 92). Actually, the Tarot is played
with a deck of seventy-eight cards, consisting of twenty-two trump cards
(Major Arcana) and four sets of fourteen suit cards (Minor Arcana). The
original four suits: Coins, Cups, Swords, and Batons. While the Coins are
sometimes depicted as pentacles or diamonds, they are not an indicator of
femininity, but rather "manifestation" or "realization." They may also be
associated with the earth and earthly things.

pentagram A pentacle enclosed in a circle. Early in *The Da Vinci Code,* Jacques Saunière's slain, nude body is disturbingly outstretched on the Louvre floor with a bloody pentacle drawn on his stomach. This image gives Robert Langdon the chance to complain about how the church has either stolen or defaced the sacred symbols and rituals of peaceful pagan religions (37).
Conversely, it was not the church that attributed negative symbolic connotations to the pentagram, but twentieth-century Satanists. The pentagram has been symbolically used by Wiccans and nature-worshiping cults since even before the writings of Eliphas Levi and Anton LaVey. See also pentacle; Star of David.

pentameter See iambic pentameter.

Pentateuch Old Testament studies term, Greek for "five vessels." Refers to the Old Testament's first five books—Genesis, Exodus, Leviticus, Numbers, and Deuteronomy. Likewise known as the Torah. See also Bible; canon; Torah.

Pépin d'Héristal Pepin II; also known as "Pepin the Fat." Dan Brown says that Dagobert II, a Merovingian king, was stabbed to death (while asleep in bed) and that his assassination was plotted by Pepin and "the Vatican" (*DVC,* 258). Dagobert II was actually killed while hunting in 679; historians believe his death was no accident, but the Vatican, as we presently know it, did not exist at that time, and there is no evidence that the pope was involved. Pepin's benefit from Dagobert's death is without question: Pépin's great-grandson was Charlemagne, and his son was Charles Martel, with whom the Merovingian dynasty was replaced by the Carolingians.

Percy, Martyn Principal of Ripon College Cuddesdon, Oxford University; was director of the Lincoln Technological Institute for the Study of Religion and Society at the University of Sheffield. His predictably unorthodox views (as evidenced in his lecture "Unconventional Thoughts on Christianity and Contemporary Culture") are frequently featured on BBC and radio programs.

pericope Rooted in a Greek word that means "a cutting." In biblical study, a short, clearly defined section, rather like a paragraph; a section of a document with a self-contained story of meaning, suitable for public reading. *Pericope* often refers to scriptural passages read aloud in a worship service.

Peter, Simon Apostle; one of Jesus' original twelve followers. According to the canonical Gospels, Peter's name was originally "Simon"; Jesus nicknamed him *Petros* (Greek, "stone") after Simon recognized Jesus as "the Christ, the Son of the living God" (Matt. 16:16–18). According to the church father Papias, Mark became Peter's translator during the apostle's journeys; Mark's gospel probably reflects Peter's eyewitness testimony. According to later tradition, Simon Peter died as a martyr after being crucified upside down.

　　The Da Vinci Code charges that the "unaltered gospels"—which allegedly include the Gnostic writings found at Nag Hammadi—prove that Mary Magdalene (not Peter) was supposed to be the church's primary leader (248). However, these texts were written more than a century after Jesus walked the earth; unlike the canonical Gospels, none of them represents eyewitness testimony about Christ's life and ministry. As such, any conflict between Peter and Mary Magdalene over the church's leadership is almost certainly pure fiction. See also *Acts of Peter;* apostle; Gnosticism; Gospels, canonical; Mary Magdalene; Nag Hammadi; Papias of Hierapolis; Roman Catholic Church.

Pharisees, The From Hebrew *perushim,* "separated ones"; Jewish social movement that began to flourish in the mid-second century BC. According to the Jewish historian Josephus, the Pharisees were one of four social groups in first-century Judaism (with Essenes, Sadducees, and Zealots). The Pharisees, who accepted as Scripture not only the Torah but also the other Old Testament books (the Prophets and the Writings), believed in a future resurrection and emphasized the importance of traditional rules ("Sayings of the Fathers" [*Pirqe Aboth*]). Even after the Pharisees ceased to exist as a social movement, the rabbis maintained their teachings, preserving many of their beliefs in the *Mishnah.* See also Bible; canon; Essenes; Josephus, Flavius; *Mishnah;* resurrection; Sadducees; Torah.

Philip IV, King (Philippe, Philip the Fair) Son of Philip III and Isabel of

Aragon (r. 1286–1314); strong-willed French king who fought various wars and engaged in innumerable intrigues. Philip imposed the power of the state upon the church, bringing him into conflict with the papacy. In response to Pope Boniface VIII's *Unum Sanctum,* King Philip sent Guilliaume de Nogaret to Italy; Nogaret's men stormed and sacked the papal quarters and held the pope prisoner for three days. Philip then manipulated the selection process to elect Pope Clement V, who moved his residence from Rome to France, ultimately settling in Avignon and launching what is known as the "Babylonian Captivity of the Church." Contrary to statements by Dan Brown (*DVC,* 159–60), it was Philip (not Clement) who took action against the Knights Templar; his main motivation was money. See also Clement V, Pope; Friday, October 13, 1307.

Picknett, Lynn, and Clive Prince Coauthors of *The Templar Revelation: Secret Guardians of the True Identity of Christ,* specifically mentioned in *The Da Vinci Code* (253). Picknett and Prince list themselves as authorities on the "paranormal, the occult, and historical and religious mysteries." *The Templar Revelation* is a staple of early-Christian-history-as-conspiracy literature.

Plantard, Pierre French fascist who did prison time for association with an anti-Semitic, anti-Masonic group called Alpha Galates; also did time for fraud and embezzlement. Plantard posed as an expert on the Knights Templar; when he was interviewed by the authors of *Holy Blood, Holy Grail,* his claims to be a Grand Master of the Priory of Sion were made public. These claims were based upon documents (called *Les Dossiers Secrets,* buried deep within the National Library in Paris) that were actually forged genealogies discreetly planted in such a way as to appear hidden. In 1993 Plantard confessed to having created both the documents and the entire Priory of Sion hoax.

Plantard and his friend Andre Bonhomme had organized the small group known as Priory of Sion, in 1956, to endorse affordable housing; they published a pamphlet entitled *Circuit* to promote their ideas. They abandoned their cause in 1957, and in the years after the breakup, Plantard created documents that would later be placed in the *Bibliothèque Nationale* as proof that a secret society guarded the identity of a royal bloodline, beginning with Mary Magdalene and Jesus and continuing through the French Merovingian kings to the present Saint-Clair family. The current descendants of Jesus supposedly included Plantard himself.

In 1989, Plantard revised some of the forged documents, adding to the list of Grand Masters the name of Roger-Patrice Pelat, a friend of French President François Mitterand. During a financial scandal involving Pelat, Plantard, called to testify, swore under oath that he had invented the Priory's entire history and existence. When the judge had his home searched, more false documents were discovered that purposed to show Plantard as the true heir to the French throne. This time Plantard was not sentenced to prison.

In 1975, Plantard had begun to associate himself with the Saint-Clair family, who were associated with the Freemasons who had built Rosslyn Chapel. This false name provided Plantard with a "bloodline" to prove he was descended from Jesus and Mary Magdalene; when he was forced to recant on the entire fabrication, this too was discounted.

Holy Blood, Holy Grail, which relied heavily upon Plantard's "evidence," served as the basis for much of Dan Brown's information concerning the Priory of Sion. See also Alpha Galates; Bibliothèque Nationale de France; *Dossiers Secrets, Les; Holy Blood, Holy Grail;* Knights Templar; Priory of Sion.

Polycarp of Smyrna Apostolic church father and martyr; d. c 160. Only one of his writings—his letter to the church in Philippi—has survived in complete form; written around 130, it's filled with quotations from the canonical New Testament, it refers to Jesus as "our Lord and God" and "the Son of God" (12:2), and it mentions his death and resurrection (1:2). Dan Brown's claim (*DVC,* 233) that Jesus was not recognized as the Son of God until the fourth century has no basis. See also apostolic fathers.

Pope, Alexander British writer; d. 1744; poet, essayist, literary critic. According to the *Da Vinci Code* conspiracy theorists, Pope belonged to a secret society known as the Rosicrucians, a supposition based on the presence of Rosicrucian themes in his 1712 poem "The Rape of the Lock." In the dedication, Pope noted that the source of any included Rosicrucian elements was "a French book, called *Le Comte de Gabalis*" that drew from "the Rosicrucian Doctrine of Spirits." Rosicrucian writings were popular

throughout Europe in the early eighteenth century; no reliable evidence
suggests that Pope's Rosicrucian involvement extended beyond this usage
of a secondary Rosicrucian source as one influence in a single poem. See
also Rosicrucians.

postmodernity Historical era beginning in the twentieth century, following
the Modern Age, during which human reason and scientific logic had
provided the framework for people to interpret their world. Modernity
assumed that if every person viewed his or her world logically, everyone
would generally come to the same conclusions. Postmodernity challenges
this assumption in maintaining that people's perceptions are *relative*—that
is, even when attempting to think logically, different minds come to different conclusions.

Unfortunately, in some cases, postmodern philosophers have concluded that since everyone perceives the world differently, there is no such
thing as truth. In this way of thinking, there is no reality; there is only
"perception" and "illusion." Viewed as such, historical sources do not
depict events that were real or true; instead, they depict "constructs" that
express the feelings of a specific person or group.

In many ways, *The Da Vinci Code* represents a literary application of
this principle. "History is always written by the winners," one of its characters claims. "When two cultures clash, the loser is obliterated, and the
winner writes the history books—books which glorify their own cause
and disparage the conquered foe" (256). This approach to historical documents is known as deconstructionism. See also deconstructionism;
modernity. (For in-depth discussions of modernity and postmodernity, see
Thomas Oden, *Requiem,* and Stanley Grenz, *A Primer on Postmodernism.*)

prelate/prelature From Latin *praelatus,* "having preferred [this person or
group]"; in the Roman Catholic Church, a person or group granted special dignity or privileges in a certain area. A *personal* prelature is a prelature over certain *persons,* in contrast to a prelature over a certain *area.* The
possibility of personal prelatures was established during the Second Vatican Council (1960s) and affirmed in the 1983 *Code of Canon Law.* Personal prelatures allowed persons to serve the Church in an order similar
to a monastic order without embracing monastic commitments to poverty
and celibacy. The first established as a personal prelature was Opus Dei,

whose members operate simultaneously under the authority of their local church and of their designated prelate. See Escrivá de Balaguer, Josemaria; Opus Dei.

prime meridian Imaginary line that runs north to south, longitudinally, marked as 0 degrees on maps and globes. In 1884, representatives of twenty-five countries meeting in the U.S. agreed upon the prime meridian's location as running through the Royal Observatory in Greenwich, England (pronounced "GREN-itch"). Previously, the Paris Meridian had been recognized as the prime, although it did not pass through the Saint-Sulpice Church as *The Da Vinci Code* claims (106).

Priory of Sion, The Dan Brown begins *The Da Vinci Code* with a page labeled "Fact," on which he describes the Priory of Sion as "a European society founded in 1099, a real organization" (1). The Priory is Brown's central focus of conspiracy, power, wealth, and historical significance; he based much of his "research" on the book *Holy Blood, Holy Grail,* in which supposedly long-undiscovered documents (*Les Dossiers Secrets*) reveal the history of this society and contain an actual list of the Priory's Grand Masters—including such men as Leonardo da Vinci, Sir Isaac Newton, and Victor Hugo (113).

In truth, the Priory was a club created in 1953 by Pierre Plantard, who later testified under oath that he had fabricated the entire hoax. The actual society existed only in the novel and in the mind of the late Pierre Plantard. See also *Dossiers Secrets, Les; Holy Blood, Holy Grail;* Plantard, Pierre.

Protestant Reformation, The See Reformation, The Protestant.

Protocols of the Learned Elders of Zion Pseudo-historical document forged by Pavel Krushevan in 1903; fake records of fictional meetings held in 1897 in Switzerland, where Jews and Freemasons supposedly gathered to plot world domination via liberalism and socialism. Although *Protocols* has been repeatedly proven fraudulent, it marks the beginning of "conspiracy-theory literature"—writings in which authors make claims that blame a certain person or group for a vast range of social problems (typically so wide-ranging and incredible that they're difficult to disprove).

Protocols first appeared in a Russian newspaper without receiving much attention. In 1905, Serge Nilus, a Czarist official, added it to a religious tract by Russian philosopher Vladimir Soloviov. Eventually *Protocols* was translated into European languages, and its notoriety began to spread, generating significant anti-Semitism; Adolf Hitler showed in his later *Mein Kampf* that he was convinced it was authentic.

In 1921, a *London Times* reporter, Philip Graves, noted its similarities with a satire written by French lawyer Maurice Joy. Additional investigation proved that *Protocols* was indubitably forged, its contents completely fictional. Nevertheless, certain groups still argue for its authenticity and promote it as proof of the threat posed by Jews and Masons.

Outrageously, *Protocols* provided the authors of *Holy Blood, Holy Grail* with supposed evidence for the Priory of Sion's existence (upon which *The Da Vinci Code*'s plot rests); they suggest that Serge Nilus possessed an original copy of *Protocols* that he altered (by adding inflammatory language) to cause the expulsion of the group he blamed for writing it. This group was allegedly a secretive circle of friends with ties to the occult and possessing favor in the court of Czar Nicholas and Czarina Alexandra. His plan failing, Nilus himself was banned from the royal court, and *Protocols* (in its altered form) survived; *Holy Blood, Holy Grail* theorizes that evidence remains within it that proves its original tie to an authentic document produced by a secretive society.

The *Protocols* signature reads, "The representatives of Sion of the 33rd Degree," which supposedly refers to a select group of Jews at the 1897 Judaic congress in Basel. The authors of *HBHG* believe that a forger would have implicated all the representatives at the congress rather than just a few, so the "33rd Degree" must apply to someone else; they conclude that this someone must be the Priory of Sion. Contributing to this conclusion are *Protocols'* references to "kingship," "king of the Jews," and "the Davidic king as pope." *HBHG* states that a real Jewish congress wouldn't be interested in kingship or the king of the Jews because those had become Christian ideas referring to Jesus; Nilus's forgery had neglected to conceal the original signature.

Those who compiled the research to prove the Priory of Sion's existence name *Protocols of the Learned Elders of Zion* as their most compelling evidence. In turn, Dan Brown acknowledges *Holy Blood, Holy Grail* as a source for *The Da Vinci Code*'s premise (253). Much of *Protocols* was plagiarized from a French satire of Napoleon III; the conclusions drawn by those who believe in the Priory are likewise false. See also *Holy Blood, Holy Grail;* Priory of Sion.

proto-orthodox Christianity In *Orthodoxy and Heresy in Early Christianity,* Walter Bauer argued that the earliest followers of Jesus didn't distinguish between "orthodoxy" and "heresy" but that, in the beginning, there were simply varying—and, sometimes, competing—forms of faith, all regarded as "Christian." The idea that one belief might be "orthodox" and another "heretical" came later, Bauer argued, probably in the fourth century. Some scholars (like Bart Ehrman) who accept Bauer's hypothesis have used the term "proto-orthodox" to refer to *pre*-fourth-century Christians whose beliefs agreed with the beliefs that would *later* become known as orthodox. See Bauer, Walter; Ehrman, Bart D.; heresy; orthodoxy.

protoevangelium From Greek *protoeuangelion,* meaning "before the gospel"; term used to describe the *Infancy Gospels.* See *Infancy Gospels.*

Protoevangelium of James, The Or *Proto-Gospel of James;* alternate title for *The Infancy Gospel of James.* See *Infancy Gospel of James.*

Pseudepigrapha Greek, meaning "falsely ascribed"; writings that claim to have been authored by those who did not actually write them. Such writings as *Book of Enoch, Gospel of Peter,* and *Gospel of Barnabas* (for instance) fit into this category.

pseudonymity The act of publishing a writing under a name other than the actual author's. Many Gnostic writings are pseudonymous—that is, they claim to be written by prominent apostles or other church leaders but were actually written by Gnostic teachers. See Gnosticism; Gospels, canonical.

Psalms Ancient book of songs found in the Old Testament Scriptures. In Protestant and Roman Catholic Bibles there are 150 Psalms; in Eastern Orthodox Bibles there are 151. See also Bible; canon.

purist documents Fictitious documents referenced in *The Da Vinci Code* (256); Dan Brown apparently based his theory on references in *Holy*

Blood, Holy Grail. Supposedly, the purist documents (also known as "Sangreal documents") include proof that Jesus married Mary Magdalene and contain a complete listing of the Priory of Sion's Grand Masters (113, 158). All of this is based on false claims and forged documents from Pierre Plantard; there is no reliable evidence that such documents ever existed. See also hidden documents; *Holy Blood, Holy Grail;* Plantard, Pierre; *Sangreal.*

Putnam, Bill, and John Edwin Wood Coauthors of *The Treasure of Rennes-le-Château,* a thorough and painstaking examination of historical bases for claims regarding Bérenger Saunière and the events at Rennes-le-Château in the late 1800s. Their work demonstrates the entire account to be a hoax.

Pyramide, La A controversial modernist entrance to the Louvre (*DVC,* 18), startlingly unlike the Renaissance palace housing the art works; seventy-one-foot glass pyramid, composed of glass, steel rods, and cables; designed by I. M. Pei; completed in 1989. *La Pyramide,* one of President François Mitterand's "grand projects," cost 6.9 billion francs to build. See also 666.

Pyramide Inverse, La Suspended like a stalactite from the ceiling of the Carrousel du Louvre, a shopping mall in front of the museum, is *La Pyramide Inverse*—I. M. Pei's Benedictus Award–winning inverted pyramid, an upside-down version of the large pyramid outside (*DVC,* 22, 453–54). Completed in 1993, a glass skylight whose tip descends to 1.4 meters above the floor; under it is a small stone pyramid resting on the floor, and their tips almost meet. Dan Brown sexualizes the inverted pyramid's meaning, claiming it represents the chalice, the eternal feminine as featured in *The Da Vinci Code;* find-

ing symbolic genitalia in architecture and art, he claims the small stone pyramid is the masculine "blade," a phallic symbol.

The crescendo of the novel is that the small pyramid (so Brown says) is merely the crest of a larger pyramid, a sarcophagus containing the body of Mary Magdalene and secret documents concerning her. Brown's imagination knows few limits, which can be a good thing for a novelist unless you have begun your story with the word *fact.* The supposed Magdalene burial site pushes the literary envelope beyond plausibility.

Q From German *quelle,* "source"; New Testament studies term. According to *The Da Vinci Code,* Q is a hidden document, "a book of Jesus' teachings, possibly written in his own hand." The truth is, some scholars propose the existence of a document simply called "Q" (which has never been found) in attempting to explain why so many of Jesus' teachings in the gospels of Matthew and Luke are similar, yet not identical. The idea is that as the authors wrote, they used a common document, now lost, that had summarized Jesus' teachings. Even if this document did exist at some point, its contents were far from scandalous; it was simply Christ's teachings as related by both Matthew and Luke. If Luke used Matthew as a source—which is quite possible—then Q is not needed as an independent document. (See Mark Goodacre and Nicholas Perrin, eds., *Questioning Q: A Multidimensional Critique* [Downers Grove, IL: InterVarsity Press, 2004].) See also deconstructionism; L source; M source; redaction criticism.

Quest for the Historical Jesus, The See Schweitzer, Albert.

Qumran Settlement near the Dead Sea; nearest village to the caves where the Dead Sea Scrolls were discovered. See Dead Sea Scrolls; Essenes.

redaction criticism Subfield of form criticism; study of the reasons different sources might have been joined in certain ways ("redacted") to form a
single work. See form criticism.

Reformation, The Protestant Sixteenth-century movement in which theologians and ministers attempted to reform the Roman Catholic Church's
theology and practice. Although the groundswell had begun earlier, Martin Luther's posting of his *Ninety-five Theses* in Wittenberg in 1517 is
usually seen as marking the Reformation's beginning.

   Luther questioned the pope's power and also the concept of indulgences. (According to medieval Roman Catholic theology, "indulgences"—which could be earned, bought, or sold—freed a person from
sin's temporal consequences.) The pope's response to Luther's protest
demanded that he retract his ideas. In 1521, the "Holy Roman Emperor"
summoned Luther to recant before an imperial gathering (a *diet*) in the
village of Worms; Luther refused to recant unless someone convinced him
"by Scripture or by evident reason" that he was mistaken. The emperor
then granted Luther safe-conduct to return home; however, Frederick the
Wise, elector of Saxony, knowing that Luther would become a wanted
man, kidnapped Luther and hid him in Wartburg Castle. There Luther
produced a vibrant German translation of the New Testament. The following year he emerged from hiding; within a decade, leaders such as
Ulrich Zwingli, John Calvin, and John Knox had joined him in his call
for reform. In the end, the result was not a reformation of the established
church, but a division of it, first into Catholic and Protestant branches
and then into other sects (such as Lutheran, Reformed, and Anabaptist)
that remain to this day. See also Holy Roman Empire; Roman Catholic
Church.

Renaissance, The Literally means "rebirth"; traditionally, the cultural movement in Italy during the fourteenth and fifteenth centuries; the term has also been used to describe the transitional period between the Middle Ages (fifth through fourteenth centuries) and has also been applied to Modern Europe, which historians say began with the late-eighteenth-century French Revolution. In truth, there wasn't one single unified cultural theme elevated throughout Europe, but rather many different movements influenced by the art, writings, and scientific developments inspired through the revival of classical cultures, dissatisfaction with the Roman Catholic Church, and the rise of philosophical humanism (the centrality of self and its potential).

Most scholars agree that Florence was the origin of the Italian Renaissance. Church corruption and abuses by parish priests caused some intellectuals to turn from religion to humanism, glorifying humanity and demanding respect and dignity for all people, regardless of social status, race, or creed. This shift toward secularism was also seen in literature, art, and science; Latin had been the language most used by educated writers, but the Florentines Dante Alighieri ("the father of modern Italian"; d. 1321) and Boccaccio (d. 1375) produced classic writings in contemporary vernacular. The great poet Geoffrey Chaucer (d. 1400) subsequently wrote *Canterbury Tales* in English.

By the time Leonardo da Vinci was born in 1452, Florence had an energized economy and a large group of erudite and wealthy people supporting the arts and scholarship. Leonardo is often called the true "Renaissance Man" because he was successful and influential in a mind-bending variety of artistic and scientific fields. During the Italian Renaissance, thinkers and artists like Petrarch (d. 1374), Michelangelo (d. 1564), Raphael (d. 1520), and Machiavelli (d. 1527) were given intellectual freedoms and monetary support resulting in remarkable cultural achievements that eventually affected the entire European community.

Rennes-le-Château Small community in Southern France not directly mentioned in *The Da Vinci Code* that plays a prominent background role and is also mentioned in *Holy Blood, Holy Grail*. It was here that conspiracy theorists contend Bérenger Saunière allegedly found papers related to the Priory of Sion. See Corbu, Noël; Putnam, Bill and John Edwin Wood.

resurrection Translation of the Greek *anastasis*, literally "standing anew"; complete renewal of life within a formerly deceased body. Unlike belief in reincarnation or in the soul's immortality, resurrection assumes the essential unity of an individual's physical and spiritual aspects; therefore, the authors' accounts of Christ's resurrection in the canonical Gospels cannot have been intended merely to describe a spiritual awareness among them of his continuing presence. (See N. T. Wright, *The Resurrection of the Son of God* [2003] for a brilliant defense of Christ's physical resurrection.) See Christology.

Roman Catholic Church, The The church that recognizes the Bishop of Rome as the visible source of Christian unity and as the apostle Peter's successor. According to Roman Catholic interpreters, Jesus granted a unique measure of authority to Simon Peter (see Matt. 16:13–19). As the primary leader of the church in the city where Peter died, the Bishop of Rome—the pope—is viewed as the divinely ordained trustee of this authority.

The adjective *catholic* appears as a description of the church in the writings of several early church fathers, including Ignatius. In these writings, the word did not refer to a specific group of Christians; *catholic* meant "worldwide" or "universal," referring to the universal agreement among all true Christians concerning essential beliefs.

Beginning in the second century, the Roman bishop's claims of supreme authority in the church became a source of conflict between Christians in the western and eastern halves of the empire. In this context, the adjective *Roman* began to distinguish congregations that accepted the Roman bishop's authority. This conflict—coupled with the pope's excommunication of Eastern Christians (in 1054) and the sacking of Constantinople (in 1204)—ultimately divided the Eastern Orthodox Church from the Roman Catholic Church.

In the fourteenth century, the "Babylonian Captivity" of the papacy (1309–1378) and the Great Papal Schism (1378–1417) disgruntled many Catholics, and the corruption of Renaissance popes deepened their discontent. When Martin Luther protested the sale of indulgences, these elements erupted in the events now known as the Protestant Reformation.

The Catholic Council of Trent (counterreformational; 1545–1563) responded to the charges brought by the Reformation in affirming that

Scripture and church tradition are both authoritative, that good works are necessary for salvation, and that Jesus ordained seven sacraments; they also attempted to end the Reformation-triggering abuses of power. The Trent decisions defined Roman Catholic beliefs and practices for more than four hundred years.

In 1962, Pope John XXIII convened the Second Vatican Council to accomplish *aggiornamento* (Italian, "updating") in the Church. The council allowed for the translation of the Mass into native languages and recognized that believers outside the Roman Catholic Church can be Christians. Even with Vatican II's changes, certain aspects of Catholic theology remained unchanged: it still regards good works as essential for justification, the Blessed Virgin Mary receives reverence as Mother of the Church, *theotokos* (Greek, "bearer of God"), and the bishop of Rome is still understood to be the supreme representative of Christ's presence and power.

Although Roman Catholic history includes its share of dark shadows, *The Da Vinci Code* is filled with claims about Catholicism that are completely false or, at the very least, questionable. For example:

- The Church "launched a smear campaign against the pagan gods and goddesses, recasting their divine symbols as evil" (37). In fact, Roman Catholic missionaries to pagan peoples usually tried to maintain the pagans' "divine symbols" by giving them new meanings—meanings that called attention to the God of the Scriptures.
- "The fundamental Catholic doctrine [is] that of a divine Messiah who did not consort with women or engage in sexual union" (257). Although Roman Catholic theology does proclaim a divine Messiah who lived a celibate life, this is far from *the* fundamental Catholic doctrine.
- Jesus was declared divine at the Council of Nicaea to solidify "the new Vatican power base" (233). Actually, the Vatican as we know it didn't even exist when the Council gathered in 325. Furthermore, nearly all attending representatives came from the Eastern (Byzantine) half of the empire, with very little representation from the Western (Roman) portion. Most important, Christians throughout the world viewed Jesus as divine in the first century, more than two hundred years before Nicaea.
- Certain "members of the Catholic clergy" would be willing to engage

in murder to suppress supposed evidence that Jesus married Mary Magdalene (266; see also 254)—a charge for which there is no reliable evidence.

- The Church demonized human sexuality because "mankind's use of sex to commune directly with God posed a serious threat to the Catholic power base" (309). Some early Christian theologians did exhibit negative attitudes toward human sexuality, but these attitudes stemmed primarily from the widespread influence of Platonism, the philosophy undergirding Gnosticism. No evidence suggests the early church engaged in a concerted effort to "demonize" human sexuality. See also Council of Nicaea; Crusades; Gnosticism; Ignatius of Antioch; Inquisition; Mary, mother of Jesus; Opus Dei; Peter, Simon; Renaissance.

Roman empire, The Politico-historical entity, originally centered in the city of Rome, lasted from 31 BC until AD 476. In the fourth and fifth centuries, the empire's power base moved from the Western half, centered in Rome, to the Eastern; during the reign of Constantine, the village of Byzantium (later renamed "Constantinople") became the capital. Increasingly, Germanic tribes—popularly known as "barbarians"—migrated in from the west, and the city of Rome became more a symbol than an actual center of power. In 476 it fell to the chieftain Odovacer, and the empire as once known ceased to exist. See also Constantine the Great; Greco-Roman world; Holy Roman Empire.

Romanticism Broad-reaching term most often referring to early-nineteenth-century Western culture, greatly influenced by changing political regimes and philosophical movements. Large-scale events like the American and French Revolutions had been ushering in the governments of the modern world, and a sense of equality and freedom was replacing the monarchies and traditions of the Middle Ages. The Romantics extolled human achievements and potential, the beauty of the natural world, and often embraced Enlightenment philosophies (such as free reason, upward human progress, and the value of all human life). Literature and music were filled with emotion and were sometimes used to make bold political statements.

The French Romantics included Victor Hugo and Alexandre Dumas; in Germany the Romantic period produced the compositions of

Beethoven and the writings of Kant and Goethe; in England the Romantic writers included William Blake, William Wordsworth, Lord Byron, Samuel Taylor Coleridge, and John Keats, among many others.

rose as symbol In *The Da Vinci Code,* the rose is a complex symbol that represents the Holy Grail, Venus, womanhood, direction, and secrets, (202); even more specifically, the five-petal rose is said to represent the various stages of a woman's life cycle as well as her physical appearance (254–55). Clever as a literary device that attractively connects many themes within the novel, the rose has been widely and broadly used as a symbol for thousands of years, so its meanings also aren't limited to those listed above.

Rose Line, The *The Da Vinci Code* describes the Rose Line as an invisible straight line, drawn from the North Pole to the South Pole, that represents the original prime meridian (0 degrees longitude, before it was chosen to run through Greenwich, England). According to Dan Brown, the Rose Line passed right through the Church of Saint-Sulpice in Paris, over the brass line on its floor (105). Actually, that line passed by this church over one hundred meters to the east. See prime meridian.

Rosicrucians, The German tradition says that Christian Rosenkreuz, after returning to Germany following years of world travel, founded "the Fraternity of the Rosie Cross," a secret group that created a unique language and traveled widely, doing good deeds for persons in need; they were also believed to have published works supporting Protestant ideas. It was later discovered that the Rosicrucians as such never existed—the fraternity was a hoax perpetrated by Johann Valentin Andreae, a Lutheran pastor.

One of the most enduring Rosicrucian texts was the *Chemical Marriage of Christian Rosenkreutz,* in which the grail seeker endures a series of tests to prove his worth. The eighteenth century saw the founding of a group supposedly focused on the works of Andreae but actually focused more on alchemy. Rosicrucian groups today tend to be about spiritual guidance rather than organized religion; one of the largest in the U.S. is called the Ancient and Mystical Order Rosae Crucis (AMORC), which meets in San Jose, California (*DVC,* 195).

Rosslyn Chapel In 1450, William Sinclair, Earl of Orkney, began construction on the Rosslyn Collegiate Church outside the small village of Roslin, Scotland; his second-oldest son, Oliver, seems to have been responsible for its completion. The original plans are lost, so it's not clear if Sinclair intended for additions to the chapel, and there's no explanation of the building's elaborate ornamentation. As for Solomon's temple being its inspiration, the model for the chapel's  floor plan can be found a few miles away at the Glasgow Cathedral.

Around 1600, another William Sinclair, descended from the former, became a patron of the Masons. Eventually, the Sinclairs became Scottish Freemasons, and mystery surrounding the guild prompted speculations about Rosslyn Chapel. No connections between Rosslyn and the Templars were conjectured before the nineteenth century.

The church's name comes from its location on a promontory (*ross*) and the nearby River Esk (*lynn*), not from its supposed position upon the north-south meridian passing through Glastonbury (*DVC*, 432–33). The chapel's latitude is 55° 85° N; Glastonbury sits at 51° 09° N. Contemporary searches for caverns beneath the chapel have been fruitless; it is doubtful that the chapel would survive excavations beneath its foundation. See also *Boaz* and *Jachin*. See map of Roslin, Scotland, page 203.

Sabbath From Hebrew *shabbat,* "rest"; seventh day of the week, designated as a day of rest in the Jewish Scriptures (Gen. 2:1–3; Ex. 20:8–11). According to *The Da Vinci Code,* "Originally . . . Christianity honored the Jewish Sabbath of Saturday, but Constantine shifted it to coincide with the pagan's veneration day of the sun" (232–33). In fact, Christians began first-day worship in the first century (see Acts 20:7; 1 Cor. 16:2). *Didache,* a church manual penned in the late first or early second century, states that Christians worshiped on "the Lord's Day," referring to the week's first day, the day of the Lord's resurrection (Matt. 28:1; Mark 16:2; Luke 24:1; John 20:1).

The third-century writings of Hippolytus suggest that many early Christians worshiped on Saturday *and* Sunday (*Apostolic Constitutions,* 23). This practice continued until the fourth century, and Constantine had nothing to do with ending it; in 365, the Council of Laodicea voted to end Saturday/Sunday worship, nearly thirty years after his death. The Council's rationale seems to have been a desire to draw a clear distinction between Judaism and Christianity. See also *Didache;* Hippolytus.

sacred feminine Dimensions of divinity that exhibit female qualities, especially motherhood (*DVC,* 23). The recent popularity and promotion of sacred feminine comes from those who claim that male-dominated societies have sought to eliminate the feminine aspects of the divine to suppress women. In *The Da Vinci Code,* Robert Langdon accuses the Roman Catholic Church of creating a smear campaign against Mary Magdalene in order to exclude women from church leadership (238). Many advocates of sacred-feminine religion ignore or discount the abundance of female figures extolled in Judeo-Christian writings and the many teachings of Jesus requiring followers to treat all people with love and respect. Worship of the sacred feminine is based on self-exploration and finding holiness from within, in opposition to the Creator being distinct from creation.

Sadducees From Hebrew *tsedduqim,* "followers of Zadok," a high priest who anointed King Solomon; flourished from the mid-second century BC until the late first century AD; according to Josephus, one of the four social groups in first-century Judaism (Essenes, Pharisees, and Zealots). The Sadducees denied a physical resurrection, accepted only the Torah as inspired Scripture, and were connected closely to the temple leadership. When the temple was destroyed in AD 70, the movement ceased to exist. See also Essenes; Pharisees; resurrection; temple, Herod's; Torah.

Saint-Sulpice Parisian church constructed from 1646 to 1780 (a church of the same name had been on the site since the twelfth century); design is similar to Notre-Dame de Paris, although smaller. There is no evidence the church is built upon ancient Roman ruins; this *Da Vinci Code* claim (54, 107) caused church officials to post a statement that Saint-Sulpice is not a pagan temple. A seminary was established  nearby in 1649, but no building is attached to Saint-Sulpice (88), and the seminary is for priests, not nuns. As with many European Catholic churches, there are no pews (89, 104) or kneeling rails in the sanctuary; nor is there a choir balcony to hide someone keeping an eye on mysterious guests (90).

The Saint-Sulpice Obelisk (115) is a tall, slender monument in the sanctuary, placed there under the instructions of Languet de Gergy (d. 1750). During the vernal equinox, a window allows sunlight to strike the copper line that runs down the obelisk, marking the accurate date of Easter. This line has never been associated with the Rose Line (as *The Da Vinci Code* says), nor does it coincide with the Paris meridian, located a hundred meters away.

Saintes-Maries-de-le-Mer, Les One *Da Vinci Code* character weaves a fascinating tale about the fate of Mary Magdalene following the crucifixion—a conglomeration of legends that have emerged throughout the centuries. (There is no written record of what happened to Mary.) This story combines the theory that Joseph of Arimathea rescued Mary Magdalene from persecution and took her to France with the local legends of the resort town Les Saintes-Maries-de-le-Mer—originally a small fishing village along the Mediterranean.

Mary Magdalene supposedly traveled across the sea from Jerusalem and landed here. Mary Jacobe (mother of James, and the sister of the Virgin Mary), Mary Salome (mother of the apostles James and John), and their servant, Sarah, were also in the boat. Mary Magdalene and Lazarus are said to have preached in Marseilles before Mary retired to a mountainous cave; locally, her bones were believed to have been discovered in 1279 in St. Maximin la Ste Baume; there her remains, according to this legend, have been protected by the Dominican monks, and thousands of pilgrims visit each year. See also Notre Dame-de-la-Mer.

Sangreal *The Da Vinci Code* contains many word plays that add fun and mystery to its plot; the twists made with *Sangreal* are clever but inaccurate (46, 160). Supposedly, the French word for "Holy Grail" is derived from the ancient words *sang real,* translated to mean "royal blood" (250). However, legends about the existence of a grail did not originate until the medieval stories of Arthur and his knights were created; in these works the term was *Sankgreall,* and the term "grail" comes from the Latin *gradale,* which means "platter." In Chretien's poem *Perceval* (from 1170), the grail was thought of as a flat dish, not a chalice. (The literal translation of "royal blood" into French would be *le sang royal,* which, as a native of France, the fictional Sophie would know.) On the "Sangreal" documents Dan Brown references (256), see hidden documents; purist documents; see also *Holy Blood, Holy Grail;* Holy Grail; Knights Templar.

Santa Maria delle Grazie Site of Leonardo da Vinci's *The Last Supper;* refers to both the church and the Dominican monastery constructed between 1466 and 1490 in Milan, Italy. The Duke of Milan, Ludovico Sforza, designated it the official court church; in 1495 he commissioned Leonardo to paint murals upon the refectory (dining hall) walls. Leonardo's slow progress resulted in only the one mural. The wall facing *The Last Supper* displays a painting entitled *Crucifixion,* done by Giovanni Donato Montorfano in 1495.

Saunière, Bérenger Priest assigned to the French village of Rennes-le-Château in 1885; a poor man who became moderately wealthy selling Masses; unethical behavior caused his suspension as priest in 1911; source of wealth came under speculation; eventually became the central figure in Pierre Plantard's Priory of Sion hoax.

Holy Blood, Holy Grail claims Saunière discovered documents in his church that contained such important information that he gained immediate wealth and prestige. A succinct summary of this mystery was given on NBC's *Dateline* (4/13/05) by commentator Stone Phillips: "If you're wondering how the priest, Saunière, amassed that mysterious fortune, well, it had nothing to do with unearthing secrets about the Holy Grail. It turns out he was accused of selling mail order prayer services for the dead, a scandal that got him suspended from the pulpit. And it appears all other explanations of the mystery are simply fiction." Archaeologist Bill Putnam and engineer John Edwin Wood, evaluating all historical considerations in their exhaustive study *The Treasure of Rennes-le-Château,* show "how insubstantial is the evidence" (187).

Schweitzer, Albert Twentieth-century theologian; wrote the controversial *Quest for the Historical Jesus* (1906). When Schweitzer employed the methods of historical and literary criticism to discern the real, "historical" Jesus described in the New Testament, he proposed that his interpretation stood in contrast to the theological "Christ figure" the Christian community has found in those same texts. Not surprisingly, Schweitzer's "scientific" approach to documents of faith left him discouraged; he abandoned theology completely.

scroll Rolled sheet of writing material most commonly used before the first century AD. See also codex; manuscript; papyrus.

Secret Book of James, The Also known as *Secret Gospel of James;* late-first or second-century Gnostic writing discovered at Nag Hammadi; claims James, brother of Jesus as its author. James, also known as James the Just, was stoned to death in AD 62; furthermore, the author does not seem to have accepted a physical resurrection, while the earliest Christians viewed physical resurrection as an essential belief (see 1 Cor. 15:3–19). In *Secret Book of James,* Jesus is buried in the sand, and resurrection is never mentioned. No early Christian writer considered this document to have any authority for believers or any place among the canonical Scriptures, probably because it ignored resurrection and could not be clearly connected to an apostle. See apostle; canon; resurrection.

Secret Gospel of Mark, The Disputed writing; not actually a gospel, but two passages from an account of Jesus' life that, according to some scholars, appeared in an early version of the canonical gospel of Mark. In 1958, Morton Smith claimed to have discovered a lost letter, allegedly written by Clement of Alexandria, that supposedly included two quotations from a variant form of Mark's gospel. One includes these words: "In the evening a young man was coming to Jesus, wearing a linen cloth over his naked body. He remained with him that night, and Jesus taught him the mystery of God's kingdom." According to Smith, this implies that Jesus engaged in a homosexual relationship. Such claims require going far beyond what the text states; in addition, the authenticity of Smith's alleged discovery is highly questionable. Stephen C. Carlson's *The Gospel Hoax* (2005) presents evidence that Morton Smith may have forged the document. No one ever saw the document other than Morton Smith. See also Carpocratians; Gospels, canonical; Smith, Morton.

Secretariat Vaticana Fictitious Roman Catholic official in *The Da Vinci Code* who exercises control over the pope's financial and legal matters (173, 415). Somewhat similar in type to the Vatican's Secretary of State, who has no control over the finances of the pope or of the Roman Catholic Church.

Sectio Divina Latin, "Divine Division"; alternate name for Divine Proportion. See Divine Proportion.

Sénéchaux In English, plural of *Seneschal*. During the Middle Ages, the term referred to officers working directly under the lord of an estate; the role usually involved routine responsibilities, but could sometimes include the administration of justice. In *The Da Vinci Code, Sénéchaux* applies to those few who know the alleged secret of the Priory of Sion (4).

Separationist Christology Early Gnostic belief that "Jesus" and "Christ" were two separate beings. Supposedly, Christ was a pure spirit who inhabited Jesus (a human being) when Jesus was baptized. When Jesus was crucified, the Christ-spirit abandoned him; even though Jesus died, Christ lived on. "Christ," however, is a title—meaning "anointed one"—that describes Jesus' place as the long-awaited Messiah. As such, "Christ" and "Jesus" are inseparable. The apostle John wrote, "Everyone who believes that Jesus is the Christ is born of God" (1 John 5:1). See Christology; Gnosticism; Messiah.

Septuagint From Latin *septuaginta,* "seventy"; Greek translation of the Hebrew Old Testament and the Jewish apocryphal books, completed between the third and first centuries BC. The title stems from the tradition (probably false) that seventy scholars worked separately to translate, and that seventy-two days later all seventy resulting manuscripts were identical. The Septuagint gathered all important Jewish religious writings circulating during the era it was being translated. See apocrypha; canon; Old Testament.

Serapion of Antioch Christian scholar; d. 211; also known as "Scholasticus." Serapion demonstrated that *Gospel of Peter* did not belong in the New Testament canon: "We receive Peter and the other apostles just as we would accept Christ himself; but the writings that go falsely by their names we have consistently rejected, knowing that we have never received such writings as these. . . . From others who used this very gospel—I mean from the successors of those who started it, whom we call Docetists, for most of its ideas are of their school—I borrowed it, and I was able to go through it. I found that most of it belonged to the right teachings of the Savior, but there were also some additions." At least as early as the second century, Christians were concerned with guarding certain specific teachings of and about Jesus Christ; this demonstrates Dan Brown's claim that "Jesus' establishment as the 'Son of God' was officially proposed and voted on" at Nicaea in 325 is fiction (*DVC,* 233). See also canon; Docetism; *Gospel of Peter;* Gospels, canonical.

sfumato Italian term that literally means "blended"; comes from the word *fumo,* "smoky." Leonardo used it to describe a painting technique in which colors are layered upon one another to create soft, blended shadows and textures. *Mona Lisa* was painted in the *sfumato* style (*DVC*, 101).

Shekhinah (Shekinah) Hebrew, "the one who dwells"; term used by post-biblical Jewish rabbis to refer to God's glory dwelling among his people. According to Dan Brown, "early Jews believed that the Holy of Holies in Solomon's Temple housed not only God but also His powerful female equal, Shekinah" (*DVC*, 309, 446). This timeline contains a thousand-year error: early Jews didn't use the term *Shekhinah*, which doesn't appear in either Testament. Although later rabbis occasionally envisioned *Shekhinah* as a beautiful princess, *Shekhinah* was never worshiped as a deity separate from the God of Israel. See also *Adonai; Havah; Jah; YHWH*.

Shepherd of Hermas Second-century Christian apocalyptic writing that addresses the question, "How does God forgive sins committed after an individual has been baptized?" Some early Christians accepted *Hermas* as part of the New Testament canon, but the book was excluded, primarily because it could not be connected to an eyewitness of Jesus Christ. In the words of the Muratorian Fragment, written around 170: "Hermas wrote *Shepherd* very recently, in our times, in the city of Rome, while the overseer Pius, his brother, was occupying the chair of the church of the city of Rome. So it should indeed be read, but it cannot be read publicly to the people in church. For it can neither be included among the Prophets, because their number is complete, nor among the apostles, for it was written after their time." If the Muratorian timeline is accurate, *Hermas* was written between 140 and 154. See also apocalyptic; apostle; canon; Muratorian Fragment.

Sheshach A Kabbalahist tradition regards this "mysterious city" cited in Jeremiah 25:26 and 51:41 as a reference to Babel, or Babylon (*DVC*, 319).

Sibyline Oracles, The Ancient collections of supposed revelations from certain pagan prophetesses ("sibyls"). The actual oracles of the sibyls, kept in temples, were consulted only in times of gravest crisis. Because these oracles were so highly regarded, devotees of other religions—including Jews in the second century BC—created oracles in the style of the Sibylline, and later Christians followed the same pattern. No early Christian writer considered these oracles to have any authority for believers or any place among the canonical Scriptures.

666 *The Da Vinci Code,* noting the significance of the Satanic number 666, claims that French President François Mitterand ordered *La Louvre Pyramide* to be constructed with 666 panes of glass. In fact, the pyramid contains 673. ("666," coming from Revelation 13:18, is historically linked with the "beast," or Antichrist—i.e., what is antithetical to Jesus Christ.)

Smith, Morton Religious scholar who claimed to have discovered a lost letter, said to be from Clement of Alexandria, that supposedly includes two quotations from a variant form of Mark's gospel. The authenticity of Smith's supposed 1958 discovery is highly questionable, as no one ever saw the letter other than Smith. Stephen C. Carlson's *The Gospel Hoax* shows that Smith may well have forged this letter about *The Secret Gospel of Mark.* See *Secret Gospel of Mark.*

Sol Invictus, Cult of According to a Dan Brown character, Emperor Constantine "was a lifelong pagan. . . . In Constantine's day, Rome's official religion was sun worship—the cult of *Sol Invictus,* or the Invincible Sun—and Constantine was its head priest" (*DVC,* 232). This description is partly accurate. Before his claimed conversion, Constantine had been a *Sol Invictus* devotee; after he declared allegiance to Christ, Constantine seems to have seen Jesus and *Sol Invictus* as identical, perhaps resulting either from ignorance of Christian theology or as an act of political convenience, to please Christians and pagans alike. See also Christianity as "borrowed"; Constantine the Great; December 25.

Solomon's temple See temple, Solomon's.

Son of Man In the Hebrew Scriptures, "Son of Man" functions in two distinct ways. (1) Most often it means "human being" (e.g., Job 25:6; Ps. 8:4; 144:3; Isa. 51:12; Ezek. 2:1; 8:1–6; 21:2; 24:25). (2) The prophet Daniel, following a vision of God the Father ("the Ancient of Days"), sees "one like a son of man, coming with the clouds of heaven. He approached the Ancient of Days and was led into his presence. He was given authority, glory and sovereign power; all peoples, nations and men of every language worshiped him. His dominion is an everlasting dominion that will not pass away, and his kingdom is one that will never be destroyed" (Dan. 7:13–14). Accordingly, "Son of Man" can also refer to the Messiah.

When Jesus called himself "the Son of Man" (e.g., Mark 2:10–28; 8:31–38; 9:9, 12, 31; 10:33–45; 14:21, 41, 62), he was using a term that could be interpreted either as a reference to his complete humanity or to his status as Messiah. As such, perhaps he used this phrase to conceal his identity among those who misunderstood him even as he revealed his identity to those who believed. See also Christology; Jesus as Son of God.

sophia Greek, "wisdom"; in biblical usage, represents God's wisdom expressed through creation, incarnated in Jesus Christ, and imparted to believers through the Holy Spirit (e.g., Prov. 8:12–31; Luke 2:40, 52; 7:34–35; Acts 6:3, 10; 1 Cor. 1:24, 30; Eph. 1:17). In Gnostic usage, Sophia was a goddess. Many Gnostics believed that a series of paired spirits, known as *Aeons,* had emanated from "the One" (Gnostic term for the true god); Christ and Sophia were the lowest of these pairs. The Old Testament God—viewed as evil, known as "the Demiurge"—came into existence when Sophia tried to find her way back to the One without Christ, her male counterpart. See *Aeon;* Gnosticism; Separationist Christology.

Specula Vaticana Vatican Observatory, founded in 1936, located in Castel Gandolfo, a small town in central Italy. A beautiful seventeenth-century palace there, overlooking Lake Alban, serves as the pope's summer home (*DVC,* 149).

St. James Park Small London park located a few hundred yards from Westminster Abbey. The place of Rémy's murder (*DVC,* 385).

Star of David The origins of the hexagram known as the "Star of David" are unclear, but scholars believe it was first associated with astrology and, like the five-pointed star called the pentagram, it was believed to hold protective and magical powers. The star is sometimes called "King Solomon's Seal" in reference to the legendary ring from  heaven given to Solomon. The hexagon has been important to many cultures; not until the nineteenth century did it become a recognizable

symbol for Judaism. In *The Da Vinci Code,* Robert Langdon notices a hexagram worn (by foot traffic) into the floor of Rosslyn Chapel; in reality, the chapel is lined with pews that would prevent visitors from crossing the floor in straight lines (434).

Starbird, Margaret, Author of *The Goddess in the Gospels* and *The Woman With the Alabaster Jar,* which contain Dan's Brown basic theses. Both are mentioned by name in *The Da Vinci Code* (253). See *Woman With the Alabaster Jar.*

Sunday See Sabbath.

symbology The study of symbols and their meanings; *The Da Vinci Code's* Robert Langdon is a Harvard professor of religious symbology (7). For the record, no such major department actually exists at Harvard.

Synoptic Gospels, The From Greek *synopsis,* "seeing together"; refers to the first three New Testament gospels (Matthew, Mark, and Luke), which share many of the same stories about Jesus and provide a similar perspective on his life and work. See also deconstructionism; form criticism; Gospels, canonical; L source; M source; Q; redaction criticism; textual criticism.

Talmud Aramaic, "teaching"; the written traditions of the Jewish rabbis (*Mishnah*) combined with the rabbinic commentaries on these traditions (*Gemara*). See also *Mishnah*.

Tarot *The Da Vinci Code* says the Tarot cards were originally created to convey secret teachings about the Holy Grail (92, 253, 391), an idea directly from Margaret Starbird's *The Woman With the Alabaster Jar*. Starbird identifies the figures depicted on the cards as specifically historical; for example, she claims the Emperor card depicts King Philip IV, who accused the Knights Templar of heresy and had them arrested; that the Pope card represents Clement V, who eventually issued the papal bull dissolving the order; and that the woman on the Empress card is Mary Magdalene. Problem: the first known deck of Tarot cards was made in 1450 and belonged to Francesco Sforza. Their purpose was entertainment; the game was played much like the modern version of Spades. The word *tarot* is derived from the Italian *tarroc,* which means "trump." Not until the eighteenth century did Tarot cards become associated with the occult. See also pentacle.

Teisch, Jessica Managing editor of *Bookmarks* magazine and author of *Da Vinci for Dummies* (with Tracy Barr), a helpful primer for the uninitiated to Leonardo da Vinci's life and work.

Templar Revelation, The Pseudo-historical writing referenced in *The Da Vinci Code* (253) as an authoritative historical account of the Knights Templar. The authors, Clive Prince and Lynn Picknett, rely heavily upon *Holy Blood, Holy Grail* and consider the foundations of their research "unassailable" (*Templar Revelation*, 48).

Temple Church, The Built in London soon after an 1128 recruiting campaign by Hugh de Payens, promoting the newly organized Knights Templar. While in London, Dan Brown's fictional characters Neveu, Langdon, and Teabing are seeking final clues about the Holy Grail; Teabing claims the church's round shape is pagan and was intended to honor the sun (*DVC*, 329, 338). On the contrary, the Temple Church modeled Jerusalem's Church of the Holy Sepulchre, built by Constantine in 335 on the site Christians believed Jesus to have been crucified. The Temple Church's original interior was most likely colorful and ornate like others of the medieval period, but during the Reformation the walls were painted white and the effigies on the floor covered. In 1840, attempts were made to restore its original condition; following bombing damage in 1941, very little of the original Temple Church remains. See map of London, page 202.

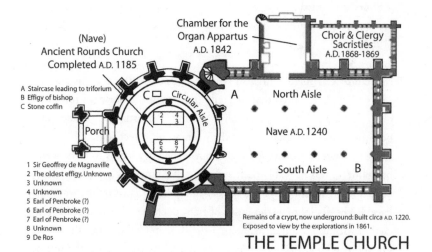

(Nave)
Ancient Rounds Church
Completed A.D. 1185

Chamber for the
Organ Appartus
A.D. 1842

Choir & Clergy
Sacristies
A.D. 1868-1869

A Staircase leading to triforium
B Effigy of bishop
C Stone coffin

Circular Aisle

North Aisle

Porch

Nave A.D. 1240

South Aisle

1 Sir Geoffrey de Magnaville
2 The oldest effigy. Unknown
3 Unknown
4 Unknown
5 Earl of Penbroke (?)
6 Earl of Penbroke (?)
7 Earl of Penbroke (?)
8 Unknown
9 De Ros

Remains of a crypt, now underground: Built circa A.D. 1220.
Exposed to view by the explorations in 1861.

THE TEMPLE CHURCH

temple, Herod's Not a new Jewish temple, but a renovation and expansion of the temple reconstructed at the urging of Zerubbabel and Haggai between 535 and 515 BC (Ezra 2–6; Haggai 2). Herod the Great began his renovations around 19 BC; they continued for eighty-two years, and the Romans destroyed it in AD 70, only seven years after its completion (*DVC,* 158). See Josephus, Flavius; temple, Solomon's.

temple, Solomon's Constructed around 1000 BC, the first built for the God of Israel; destroyed by the Babylonians in 586 BC. According to Dan Brown, Jewish men used Solomon's temple to engage in *Hieros Gamos* (*DVC,* 309); the Old Testament, however, specifically expresses God's displeasure with those seeking deeper divine experiences through ritualistic sex, referring to them as "cult prostitutes" (Deut. 23:17). When the Israelites did allow ritualistic sex around their temple (1 Kings 14:24), righteous kings such as Josiah destroyed their structures (2 Kings 23:7; 2 Chron. 34:33; cf. 1 Kings 15:12; 22:46). See *Hieros Gamos;* temple, Herod's.

Templiers sont parmi nous, Les French phrase meaning "The Templars are among (or with) us"; also the title of a book by Gerard de Sede (1962).

Tertullian of Carthage Christian scholar; d. 230; became a Christian in 197 or 198; later stated that he could not imagine a Christian life without a definite point of conversion, declaring, "Christians are made, not born." In 207, Tertullian joined the Montanists, a sect some Christians viewed as heretical, although their known theology seems to have been orthodox. It was probably their strictness that attracted Tertullian; he once said, "You can judge the quality of a person's faith by the way he lives. Right discipline is the index of right doctrine." Because of his association with the Montanists, neither the Roman Catholic nor the Eastern Orthodox Church has ever declared him a saint. Tertullian is the source of the now-famous quote, "The blood of the martyrs is the seed of the church." See also church fathers.

Testament of Levi, The Late-second-century-BC Jewish writing; found among the Dead Sea Scrolls; an apocalypse describing a vision in which the "heavens were opened" and an angel conducted the writer into heaven's first level. No early Christian writer considered this document to have any authority for believers or any place among the canonical Scriptures. See also apocalyptic; canon; Dead Sea Scrolls.

Testament of Moses, The First-century-AD Jewish writing; presented as the last words of Moses to Joshua; written many centuries after Moses' death. Jude 9 may refer to a now-lost ending of *Testament of Moses,* often referred to as *Assumption of Moses.* This would not necessarily indicate that Jude viewed it as part of the biblical canon; rather, that the quoted portion represented a true and authentic Jewish tradition. No early Christian writer considered this document to have any authority for believers or any place among the canonical Scriptures. See also apocrypha; canon; *Enoch, Book of;* pseudepigraphica.

Testaments of the Twelve Patriarchs Late-second-century-BC Jewish writing; presented as the last words of Jacob to his twelve sons; actually written during the reign of the Maccabeean king John Hyrcanus, whom it depicts as the Messiah. In the first century AD, one or more Christian writers altered the document to depict Jesus as Messiah; this version appears in the Old Testament of the Armenian Orthodox Church. Outside its usage among the Armenian Orthodox, no early Christian writer considered this document to have any authority for believers or any place among the canonical Scriptures. See also apocrypha; canon; Maccabees; Messiah.

Tetragrammaton Greek, "four letters"; reference to *YHWH,* the personal name of God that Jews would not utter lest they speak his name in vain. Dan Brown clearly misunderstood this term (*DVC,* 309). See *YHWH.*

textual criticism Also known as lower criticism; subfield of the study of ancient texts; study of manuscript copies with the goal of determining the original manuscript's (the "autograph's") wording. See also autograph; manuscript.

Thecla Legendary martyr; a virgin mentioned in *The Acts of Paul and Thecla,* which is primarily fictional, although Thecla's martyrdom may be based on an actual historical event. See *Acts of Paul and Thecla.*

Theodosius I (the Great) Roman emperor, d. 395; issued a series of decrees in 391 declaring Christianity the official religion of the empire. According to *The Da Vinci Code,* Emperor Constantine made Christianity the empire's official religion (232); Constantine did use the empire's power to support certain segments of Christianity, but he never declared it the state religion. See Constantine the Great.

Theosophy Refers to the belief that all spirituality and all religions are valid because divinity can be expressed in an infinite number of ways. Adherents claim that Theosophy's origins can be traced to the beginnings of time, but the official organization was founded by Madame Helena Blavatsky in 1875. The Theosophical Society maintains reincarnation, karma, and the power of the human mind affect reality.

Theotokos Greek for "god-bearer" or "Mother of God"; a title assigned by the early church to Mary, the mother of Jesus, at the Third Ecumenical Council held at Ephesus in 431. The theological significance at the time was to emphasize that Mary's son, Jesus, was fully God as well as fully human, and that Jesus' two natures (divine and human) were united in a single person of the Trinity. The competing view, that Mary instead should be call *Christotokos,* meaning "Mother of Christ," was advocated by Nestorius, Patriarch of Constantinople; the opposition's intent was to restrict her role to be only the mother of Christ's humanity and not of his divine nature.

The later Council of Chalcedon (451) affirmed the decisions of Ephesus in response to an unauthorized "renegade" council a couple of years earlier, which denied that Jesus had two natures (Monophysitism). Chalcedon reconfirmed Mary as *theotokos.* See also Christology; Jesus as Son of God.

Thomas Didymus Although commonly known as "Thomas Didymus," this apostle's name was "Judas." The Aramaic title "Thomas" and the Greek term "Didymus" both mean "twin," indicating that Judas Thomas Didymus probably had a twin sibling. The canonical Gospels mention Thomas several times, not only in the listings of apostles but also in dialogues with other disciples and with Jesus; the most familiar—preserved in John 20:24–29—led to his being dubbed "Doubting Thomas." According to traditions recorded by Eusebius, Origen, and Ephrem of Syria, Thomas took the gospel into Parthia and India. Though many aspects are clearly exaggerated, he probably did take the Good News eastward and likely was martyred. Thomas was the supposed author of three post-apostolic writings, but internal and external evidences demonstrate that he didn't write any of them. See *Acts of Thomas;* Gnosticism; *Gospel of Thomas; Infancy Gospel of Thomas.*

Tjet More commonly spelled Tiet or Tyet; an Egyptian symbol for the female deity Isis (*DVC,* 23). Similar to the ankh, but with the end of the horizontal line/arms bent downward. Often placed on an Egyptian's neck at his funeral. See ankh.

Tobit Apocryphal book, accepted into the Old Testament canons of the Roman Catholic and Eastern Orthodox Churches. See apocrypha; Bible; canon.

Torah Hebrew, "Instruction" or "Law"; the first five books of the Old Testament. Also known as the Pentateuch. See Bible; canon; Pentateuch.

Treatise on Painting Collection of notes and sketches by Leonardo da Vinci. It's unclear who gathered its materials, but it seems to have been compiled over many years by various scholars. Leonardo obviously didn't intend the notes to be presented in a single volume—there is no progression of a theme or method; *Treatise* is merely a sampling of his various observations and notes about painting techniques. See Leonardo da Vinci.

Trinity, The Tenet of Christian faith that expresses the mystery implied, for example, in Matthew 28:19, where one God ("the name") is described in three persons ("of the Father, Son, and Holy Spirit"). According to Christian theology, God is one in his essence but exists in three distinct persons. See also Christology.

Tuileries Construction of Jardins des Tuileries began in 1564 by order of Catherine de Medici. After serving as home to many French rulers, including Napoleon Bonaparte, it was intentionally set on fire in 1871; its burnt shell remained standing for eleven more years until the French National Assembly demolished it. The Louvre, which was attached, remained standing and was restored. All that remains of the grand palace are its gardens, now a beautiful public park located amid four of Europe's finest museums (*DVC,* 17).

Valentinus Influential Gnostic theologian; d. 153; attempted to blend Christian theology with Greek and pagan mythologies. According to Valentinus, "Christ" was a spiritual creature (*Aeon*) who possessed the human Jesus at his baptism; this Christ-spirit then left Jesus at the crucifixion. *Gospel of Truth* is probably the work of Valentinus or one of his disciples. See also *Aeon;* Gnosticism; *Gospel of Truth;* Nag Hammadi; Separationist Christology; *sophia.*

Vatican, The Residence of the pope in Rome, situated on Mons Vaticanus; Pope Symmachus constructed the first papal residence in the late fifth century. One of *The Da Vinci Code*'s historical errors comes in stating that the Vatican suppressed Gnostic writings in the fourth century (148), during which time "the Vatican" was merely a church and cemetery, and the pope's residence was at the cathedral of St. John Lateran. Dan Brown's portrayal of Vatican Hill is approximately a thousand years premature; papal authority was posited there in the fourteenth or fifteenth century. See also Roman Catholic Church.

Venus/Aphrodite Aphrodite was the Greek goddess of love; her persona was based on the Roman goddess Venus. *The Da Vinci Code* asserts that the symbol for "female" derives from an ancient astronomical symbol for the planet Venus (36, 237). Ancient signs for goddesses (female) varied; the simple symbol portrayed in the book does not accurately represent any of them.

villain/*villes* The Latin *villanus* literally means "one who works close to the soil"; it was used in reference to serfs or peasants. Dan Brown contends that the church, fearing those who lived in rural *villes,* tied the term to "villains." This etymology is nowhere to be found in dictionaries, and there is no evidence that the church tarnished the term's meaning to imply that people from rural communities (*villes*) were wicked (villains).

Virgin/Madonna of the Rocks Painting by Leonardo, on display at the Louvre. The first of two such works by Leonardo; the second, *Virgin of the Rocks,* is oil on wood and is displayed at the National Gallery in London. In *The Da Vinci Code* (133), Sophie Neveu deciphers the anagram "So Dark the Con of Man" that her grandfather had left for her and finds a gold key behind the large painting entitled *Madonna of the Rocks.* She then uses *Madonna* as a priceless shield while being held at bay by a security guard.

Since Dan Brown states that "All descriptions of artwork . . . in this novel are accurate" (*DVC,* 1), it would seem the reader could assume that details concerning this painting are correct. Conversely, *The Da Vinci Code* contains inaccuracies about it, including its original commission and canvas size. Brown describes the painting as "five feet tall" (133), but the Louvre's own Web site records it as 198 × 123 centimeters (about 6.5 feet tall).

In 1483, Leonardo received a commission from the Confraternity of the Immaculate Conception for painted wooden panels that would contain *Madonna of the Rocks* as the center panel, God the Father over the centerpiece, and two prophets on side panels. Brown's novel explains that nuns gave Leonardo specific instructions as to the painting's contents but were unhappy with the finished work, and that Leonardo then produced for them a second, more pleasing painting, *Virgin of the Rocks* (138–39). However, at this time the Confraternity was an all-male organization; there were no nuns. Furthermore, the Confraternity's dismay was understandable, since Leonardo, for reasons known only to him, had disregarded their pointed instructions as to its contents.

Sophie describes the "explosive and disturbing details" (*DVC,* 138) as the blessing *John* seems to be giving to *Jesus,* the pointing hand of the angel Uriel, and the outstretched, threatening hand of Mary. The problem is with the identification of the characters. Sophie suggests that the child sitting with the angel is John the Baptist, but art historians have traditionally agreed that *Jesus* is closely guarded by the angel, and that it is Jesus who is giving a blessing to John.

The hand of Uriel pointing to John in the original *Madonna of the*

Rocks seems to do more compositionally than symbolically. Understanding that it is Jesus sitting by the angel explains why the child is holding up his hand in the manner of a blessing. Also, Mary's hand above the mis-identified John is nearly identical to Jesus' right hand in Leonardo's *The Last Supper*. The hand's detail and three-dimensional quality illustrate Leonardo's skill as an artist and knowledge of human anatomy. Consider-ing that Mary's hand is above *Jesus,* it may be seen as protective rather than aggressive.

Brown's unusual identification of the infant next to Uriel as John most certainly comes from a theory in *The Templar Revelation* by Lynn Picknett and Clive Prince. In this book the authors claim that Leonardo was obsessed with John and believed that he should be honored above Jesus. In addition, they say there is a secret parallel church that venerates John above Jesus and that the Templars were its protectors (*Templar Reve-lation,* 349). Perhaps the Confraternity identified this possible misinter-pretation of the infants in *Madonna of the Rocks,* and this is why Leo-nardo chose to present the characters more recognizably in *Virgin of the Rocks*. This would explain why John is shown with the traditional staff, a symbol for John the Baptist. Uriel's hand is lowered, and his eyes are directed toward John, but the movement of the painting is not as power-ful. Even so, the implications and elements of the second painting remain very close to the original, so the first could not have been *outrageously* shocking to those who commissioned it. See also *The Last Supper;* Leo-nardo da Vinci; Picknett, Lynn, and Clive Prince.

Vision of the Savior, The Late-second or early-third-century Gnostic writ-ing; known only through the fragments of *Papyrus Berlin 22220;* seems to be a Gnostic adaptation of *Gospel of Peter*. No early Christian writer con-sidered this document to have any authority for believers or any place among the canonical Scriptures. Also known as *Gospel of the Savior*. See also Gnosticism; *Gospel of Peter*.

Vision of Paul, The Alternate title for *The Apocalypse of Paul*. See *Apoca-lypse of Paul*.

Vitruvian Man Illustration by Leonardo, 1487. Early mystery in *The Da
Vinci Code* includes the puzzling way
Jacques Saunière's dead body is
arranged when discovered by the
police. Robert Langdon eventually recognizes the image Saunière had hoped
to create, interpreting the circle surrounding the body as the feminine
symbol for protection; the presence of
the male body "completed Da Vinci's

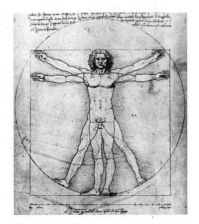

intended message—male and female harmony" (45). Clever twist, incorrect interpretation.

During the first-century reign of Caesar Augustus, Vitruvius wrote a
treatise on architecture (*De Architectura*) that established what he believed
to be perfect architectural proportions; these, he said, were applicable to
the human form. Vitruvius held that if a perfectly proportioned figure
were placed within a square whose corners were touching the boundaries
of a circle, then the exact center of both circle and square would be at the
figure's navel.

Many artists attempted and failed to illustrate this proportion; Leonardo's genius finally produced a sketch of "the well-proportioned man"
within the square and the circle. However, in *Vitruvian Man,* while the
circle is centered on the navel, the square is centered on the genitals. This
illustration was based not on male/female symbolism but on geometry.

Vulgate, The Translation of the Scriptures from Hebrew and Greek into
Latin, completed by Jerome in the early fifth century. The Latin in
Jerome's translation was "common" or "vulgar," so his rendering became
known as "the Vulgate," which remains the Roman Catholic Church's
official Latin translation. See also Jerome.

Way, The Guidebook for living, written for members of Opus Dei by its founder, Josemaria Escrivá de Balaguer; hundreds of specific directives instruct followers to work hard, to be discreet about association with Opus Dei, and to live a life of discipline and spirituality (which may include self-inflicted physical pain). The extent to which members adhere varies. See also Discipline; Opus Dei.

Wellborn, Amy Author of *De-Coding Da Vinci: The Facts Behind the Fiction of The Da Vinci Code*.

Westminster Abbey The official church for British kings and queens; the place of every royal coronation since 1066; the final resting place for historical figures like Queen Elizabeth I; a masterful work of architecture filled with rich symbols and carvings; a functioning church where services and special ceremonies are still held. The abbey is where Sophie Neveu and Robert Langdon find the final clues for the secret of the cryptex code (*DVC*, 395).

White Goddess, The Book by English poet Robert Graves (1948) expounding the goddess-worship/sacred-feminine ideas of mythology scholar Jane Harrison (d. 1928). Prior to her writings, romantic notions about a feminine earthly goddess did not exist as presented by Graves and in current pagan belief; Graves essentially created a new myth about a single goddess based upon goddess varieties named in European and Middle Eastern literature. He asserted that goddess worship traces back to the earliest human writings and that male-dominated, monotheistic tradition intentionally destroyed natural worship of the White Goddess. He also blamed the shift from worship of the feminine to the masculine as causing the modern world's chaos.

Dan Brown adopts Graves' ideas, as do contemporary goddess-worshipers. Problem: Graves failed to see that in ancient cultures, the female deity was never alone—she was always depicted and worshiped as the mate of a male deity. For the Egyptians, Assyrians, Sumerians, and Canaanites, all goddesses (many of whom were violent and cruel) had a relationship with a male deity of equal or greater power. See also goddess worship; Romanticism.

Wicca Broad religion that teaches earthly spirituality and incorporates ancient beliefs from a variety of other religions, including Celtic paganism, Greek mythology, and Egyptian idols. Founded in the 1940s by Gerald Gardner, whose writings combined ceremonies and practices from many pagan sources to create a religion that focuses upon communion with an individual's chosen god or goddess and the development of that relationship (*DVC*, 23).

Wisdom of Sirach, The Ancient apocryphal book accepted by the Roman Catholic and Eastern Orthodox Churches as part of the Old Testament canon. See apocrypha; Bible; canon.

Wisdom of Solomon, The Ancient apocryphal book accepted by the Roman Catholic and Eastern Orthodox Churches as part of the Old Testament canon. See apocrypha; Bible; canon.

witch-hunts Trials and executions of supposed witches in late medieval and early modern Europe (roughly 1250–1700). According to *The Da Vinci Code,* "during three hundred years of witch hunts, the church burned at the stake an astounding five *million* women" (125). This is a gross exaggeration. In *The Witch-Hunt in Early Modern Europe,* Brian Levack demonstrates that approximately 110,000 witch trials occurred and that about 48 percent ended in executions. Researching *Witches and Neighbors,* Robin Briggs discovered that fewer than 80 percent of these witches were women. As such, fewer than fifty thousand women were executed as witches—an undeniable and unjustifiable travesty, but a far cry from Dan Brown's claim.

Furthermore, the witch-hunts did not originate in the Roman Catholic Church, as Brown alleges. Norman Cohn (*Europe's Inner Demons*) and Richard Kieckhefer (*European Witch Trials*) found that they began among the common people of Switzerland and Croatia; the Catholic Inquisition did not become involved until the late 1400s. See Inquisition; *Malleus Maleficarum*.

Witherington III, Ben Professor of New Testament Interpretation at Asbury Theological Seminary and author of *The Gospel Code: Novel Claims About Jesus, Mary Magdalene and Da Vinci.* Witherington received his PhD from the University of Durham in England.

Woman With the Alabaster Jar, The Book cited in *The Da Vinci Code* as one of several by "historians" offering evidence that Jesus and Mary Magdalene were married and had children (253–54). Written by Margaret Starbird, who left the Roman Catholic Church after reading *Holy Blood, Holy Grail;* she attempts to equate Mary's anointing of Jesus with the sexual ritual of *Hieros Gamos,* thereby elevating her to equal status with her Bridegroom. See *Hieros Gamos; Holy Blood, Holy Grail;* Starbird, Margaret.

YHWH Hebrew; personal name of God; derived from *ehyeh* ("I Am," Ex. 3:14); also known as the Tetragrammaton. Israel viewed this name as too holy to be spoken, so, when reading the Scriptures, they substituted *Adonai* for *YHWH*. (In written Hebrew, the vowels from *Adonai* are placed with the consonants *YHWH* to remind readers.) According to *The Da Vinci Code*, *YHWH* came from the word *Jehovah* (309); in truth, *Jehovah* emerged when a sixteenth-century German translator combined *Adonai*'s vowels with *YHWH* and came up with *Yahowah* (German: *Jehovah*). See also *Adonai; Jah; Jehovah;* Tetragrammaton.

yin and yang Ancient Chinese theological concept of unclear origin; represents opposing forces present in the universe. The yin is characterized by "dark, cool, passive, earth, and female"; the yang, by its opposites, namely, "light, hot, active, heaven, and male." This dualism, a foundational tenet of Taoism, influenced the theories of Confucius. One *Da Vinci Code* character insists that Leonardo's fresco *The Last Supper* depicts Jesus and Mary Magdalene as equal, complementary divine forces, yin and yang (244).

Z

zodiac, the A development of the ancient (c. 3000 BC) Babylonian practice of astrology. Priests, observing that life was at the mercy of the weather, believed the gods lived in and controlled the heavens; in order to discern their will, cult leaders studied the positions and movements of the stars. By 130 BC, Babylonian astrology had infiltrated Greek and Roman societies and was greatly elaborated.

The imaginary celestial sphere rotates concentrically with the earth. The band located 8 degrees on either side of the path traveled by our sun is the zodiac belt, divided into twelve equal parts of 30 degrees; the sun, the moon, the planets, and constellations seen with the naked eye are in this belt. As related study became less superstitious and more scientific, *astronomy* was born. The Bible records a new star's appearance at the time of Jesus' birth, recognized by Eastern astrologers (Matt. 2:1–12). All the stars and planets of the sky were recorded in charts and monitored by astrologers.

Astrology, developing into complicated charts and maps of the constellations, continued to be used as an indicator of personalities and possible future events. Each 30-degree division of the zodiac was associated with a planet and with characteristics of the god believed to rule over that part of the sky. The signs of the zodiac are creations of ancient pagan religions and are not part of the Christian church's teachings. *The Da Vinci Code* characters believed that the Roman Catholic Church made bold moves to suppress a harmful secret as the supposed end of the Age of Pisces approached (267); this concept is outside the teachings of the faith and is not of importance to the Church. See also Age of Aquarius; Age of Pisces; astrology.

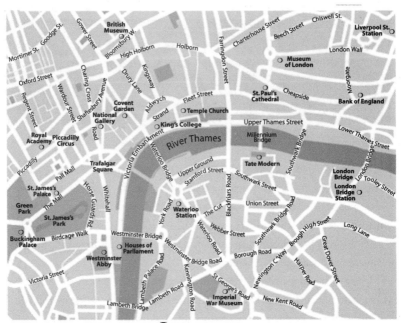

LONDON

Paris

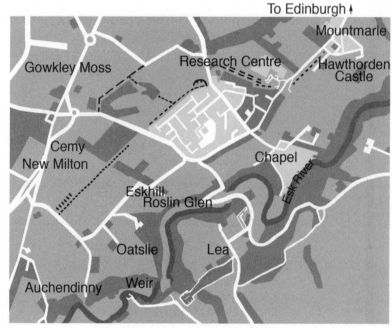

Roslin, Scotland

ABOUT THE AUTHORS

DR. JIM GARLOW is the coauthor of *Cracking Da Vinci's Code*, written with Peter Jones, which has reached half a million in print. He has Master's degrees from Princeton Theological Seminary and Asbury Theological Seminary and a PhD in historical theology from Drew University. Jim speaks nationwide and has appeared on CNN, MSNBC, CNBC, FOX, and NBC. His daily radio commentary, *The Garlow Perspective*, can be heard on nearly 500 radio outlets. He is the senior pastor of Skyline Wesleyan Church. Jim and his wife are the parents of four children and live in San Diego, California.

TIMOTHY PAUL JONES is the author of several works, including *Christian History Made Easy* and *Answers to The Da Vinci Code*. He is the recipient of the Baker Book House Award for excellence in theological scholarship and has a doctorate in educational leadership from the Southern Baptist Theological Seminary.

APRIL WILLIAMS, a professional artist, holds a Master's in theological studies from the Divinity School of Duke University. She is currently working on her PhD in early modern European history at the University of Mississippi.

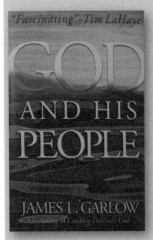
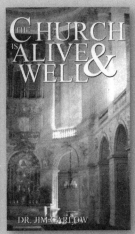
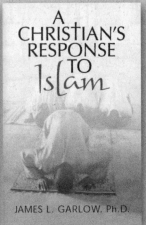
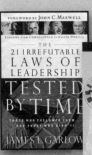

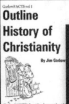

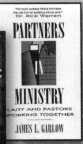